Worthington
(Art)

MAGIC EYE®

3D Hidden Treasures
by Magic Eye Inc.

Andrews McMeel Publishing

Kansas City

The material in this volume originally appeared in *Magic Eye Gallery: A Showing of 88 Images* and *Magic Eye: A New Bag of Tricks.*

ISBN: 0-7407-4791-6

Disclaimer:
The information contained in this book is intended to be educational and entertaining and is not for diagnosis, prescription, or treatment of any eye condition or disease or any health disorder whatsoever. This information should not replace competent optometric or medical care. The authors are in no way liable for any use or misuse of this material. Our wish is that further research will help to unlock the mystery of how vision and the brain work.

Magic Eye® 3D Illusions created by: Tom Baccei, Cheri Smith, Andy Paraskevas, Ron Labbe and Bill Clark (as pictured on page 118, from top to bottom).

ATTENTION: SCHOOLS AND BUSINESSES

Magic Eye® Images are available for educational, business, or sales promotional use. For information, contact:

Magic Eye Inc., PO Box 1986, Provincetown, MA 02657
www.magiceye.com

Andrews McMeel books are available at quantity discounts with bulk purchase for educational, business, or sales promotional use. For information, please write to: Special Sales Department, Andrews McMeel Publishing, 4520 Main Street, Kansas City, Mo 64111.

INTRODUCTION

Magic Eye® 3D Illusions are amazing and will challenge and entertain you. Embedded within each Magic Eye image is an enchanting 3D hidden object or scene that materializes before your eyes. Creating a Magic Eye image is a combination of advanced technology and artistic ability. Magic Eye uses its own patented algorithm. The result is a genuine MAGIC EYE® image.

When Magic Eye hit the publishing world in the 1990s, the response was as magical as the 3D images popping from their colorful backgrounds. Viewers couldn't get these best-selling books fast enough. In fact, *Magic Eye I, II,* and *III* stayed in the *New York Times* Bestseller List for 34 weeks, eventually selling more than 20 million copies with translations in more than 25 languages.

In 2001, four new Magic Eye books were released, including a best seller in Japan. *Magic Eye 3D Hidden Treasures* is the 28th Magic Eye book to be published.

In order to view Magic Eye images, you need vision in both eyes. Your eyes need to work together as a focused team. As a result, both the left and right sides of your brain are stimulated while viewing a Magic Eye image.

While Magic Eye was originally created for its entertainment value, more and more people are becoming aware of the health benefits of viewing Magic Eye images. Vision therapists and ophthalmologists worldwide have proven that viewing Magic Eye images are useful for vision therapy. Magic Eye has also become very popular with students of "whole mind" or "brain synchronization" practices, including accelerated learning, speed reading, stress management, pain management, meditation, yoga, "expanding your mind," "accessing presence," and developing your intuition. These practices focus on inducing the same state you may induce by viewing Magic Eye images.

Magic Eye images are also being used as educational tools in schools. Our images "appear" in many science and psychology school textbooks. Thousands of students use Magic Eye as a topic for papers and projects.

Magic Eye Inc. would like to take this opportunity to thank all of you for purchasing our products and for entertaining us with your letters and email. Our Magic Eye family-oriented Web site receives over 40,000 visitors a week.

If you are viewing Magic Eye for the first time, be sure to follow the viewing instructions on page four, and most importantly, have fun!

~Cheri Smith,
President, Magic Eye Inc.

www.magiceye.com

VIEWING TECHNIQUES

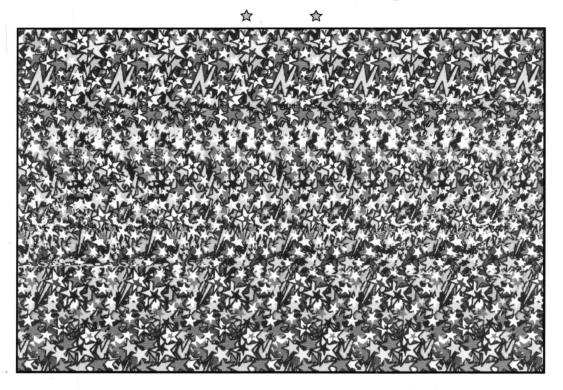

METHOD ONE

To reveal the hidden 3D illusion, hold the center of this image *right up to your nose* (it should be blurry). Stare as though you are looking *through* the image. *Very, very slowly* move the image away from your face until the *two stars* above the image turn into *three stars*. If you see four stars, move the image further away from your face until you see *three stars*. If you see one or two stars, start over! When you have three stars, *hold the image still* (if you are a beginner, try not to blink) and *the hidden image will slowly appear!* Once you see the hidden image and depth, you can look around the entire 3D image. The longer you look, the clearer it becomes!

METHOD TWO

Hold the center of the image *right up to your nose*. Stare as though you are looking into the distance. *Very slowly* move the image away from your face, perhaps an inch every two seconds. Keep looking through the page until you *begin to see depth*, then *hold the image still*. Discipline is needed when something starts to "come in" because at that moment you will instinctively try to look at the page rather than looking through it. If you "lose it," start again.

METHOD THREE

The cover of this book is shiny; hold it in such a way that you can identify a reflection. For example, hold it under an overhead lamp so that it catches the light. Simply look at the object you see reflected and continue to stare at it with a fixed gaze. After several seconds the reflection will appear to fade—let it! You will begin to perceive depth, followed by the 3D image, which will develop almost like an instant photo!

MORE INFORMATION

There are two methods of viewing our Magic Eye® images: crossing your eyes and diverging your eyes (focusing through the page at a distant focal point). All the pictures in this book were designed to be viewed by diverging the eyes. If you view the images by crossing your eyes, all the depth information comes out backward! If we intend to show an airplane flying in front of a cloud, if you cross your eyes, you will see an airplane-shaped hole cut into the cloud! Once you learn the method, try the other. Another common occurrence is to diverge the eyes twice as far as is needed to see the hidden image. In this case, a weird, more complex version of the intended object is seen.

One last note before you start. Although Magic Eye® is great fun at work and other entertaining social situations, those are often not the best places to learn. If you don't "get it" in two or three minutes, wait until another, quieter time. This technique is safe and has been proven to be helpful to your eyes, but don't overdo it. Straining your eyes will not help you "see," and will just make you feel uncomfortable. The key is to relax and let the image come to you.

The last pages of this book provide a key that shows the 3D picture that you will see when you find and train your MAGIC EYE®.

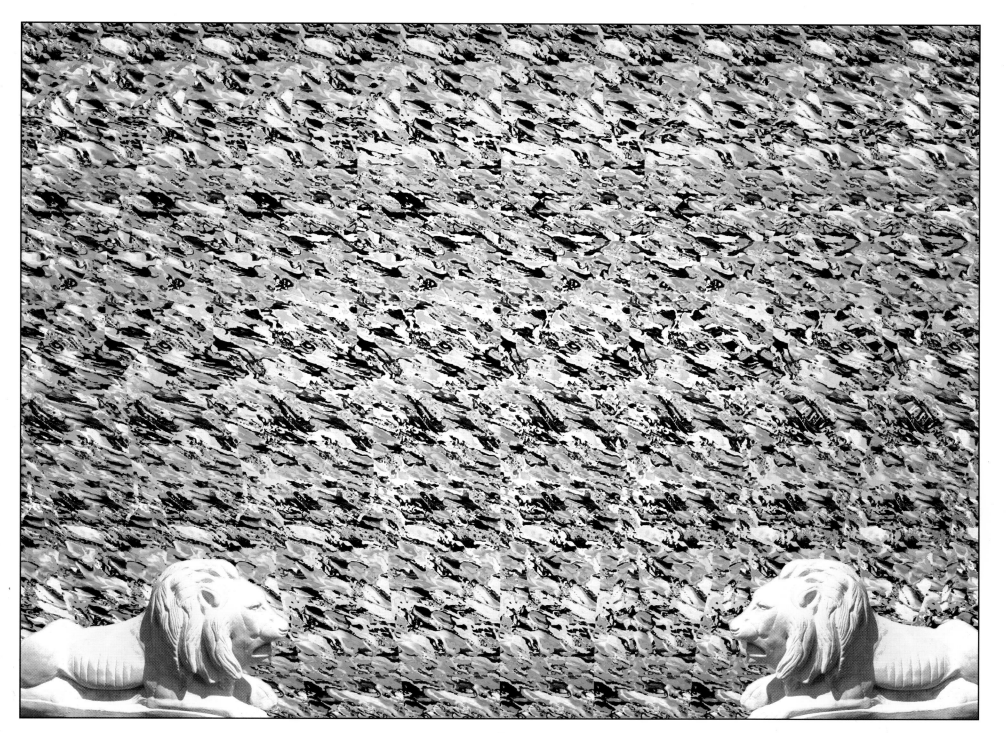

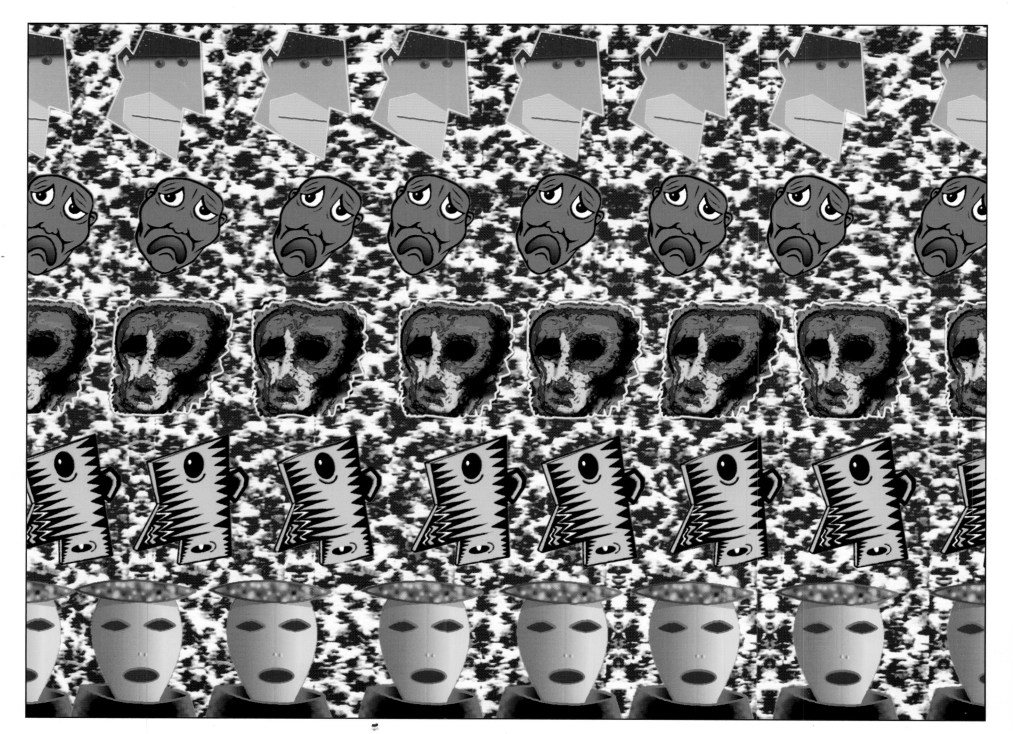

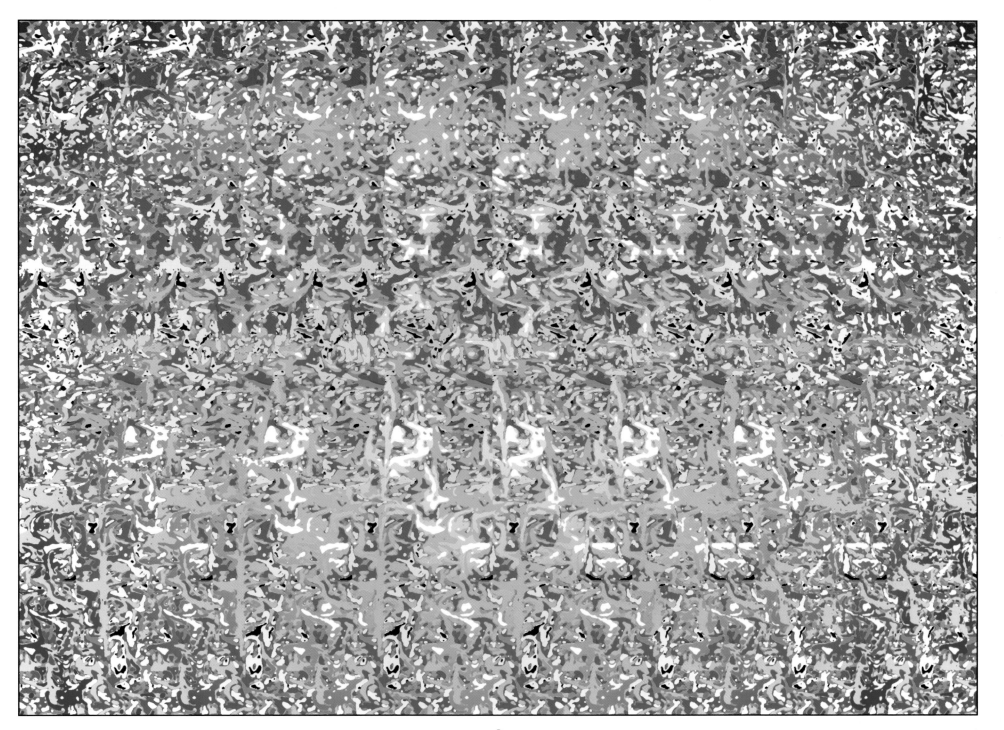

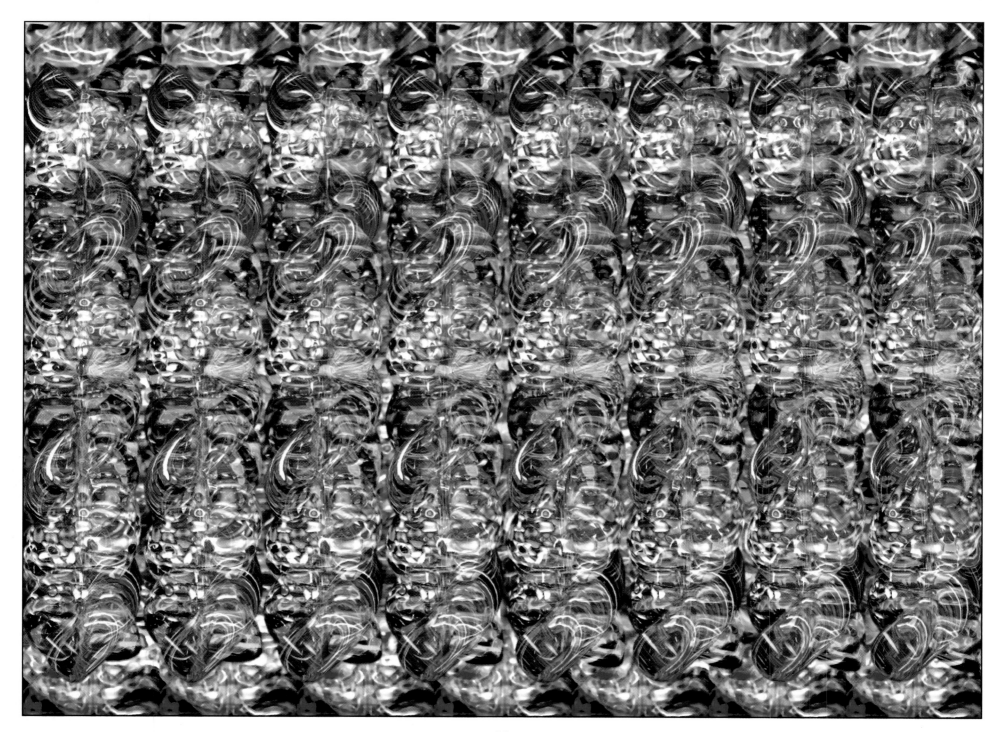

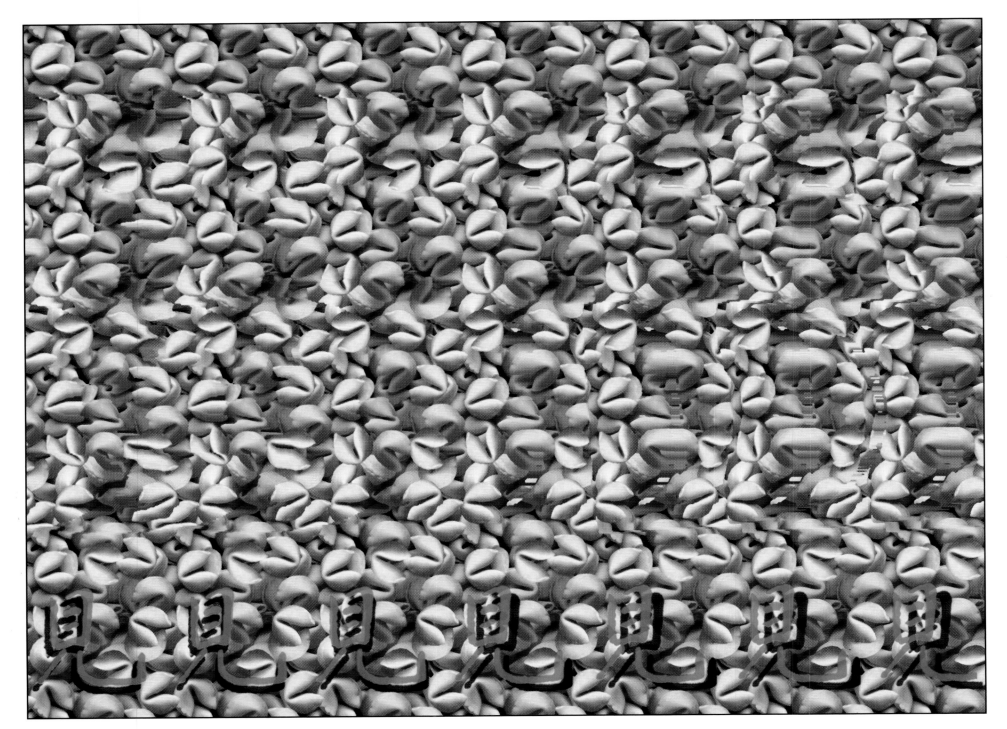

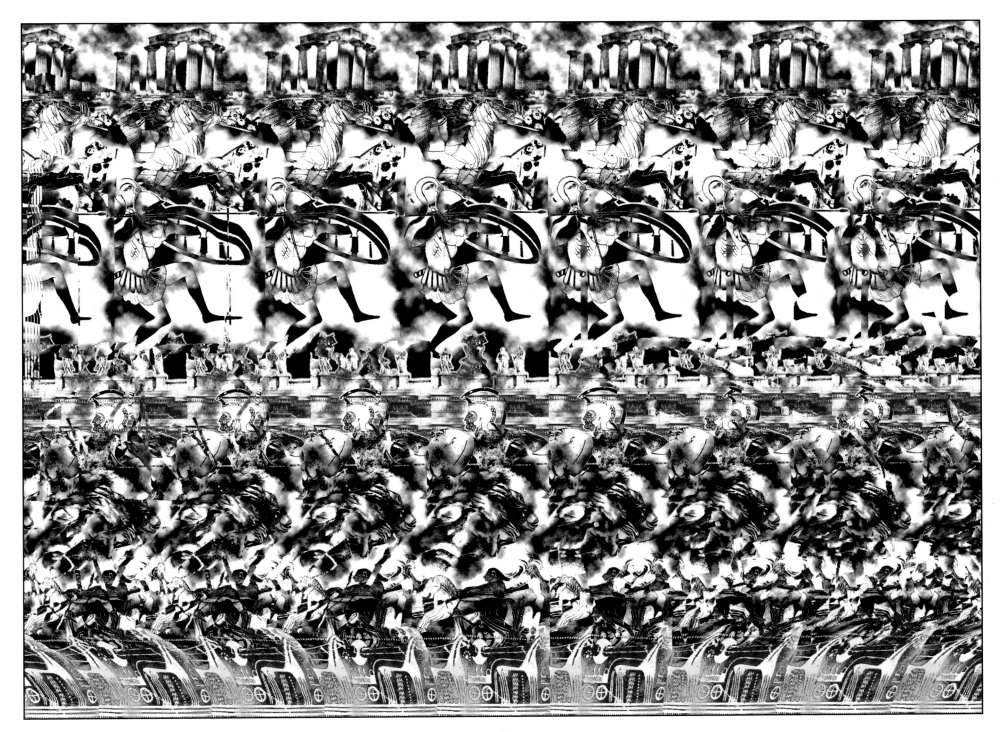

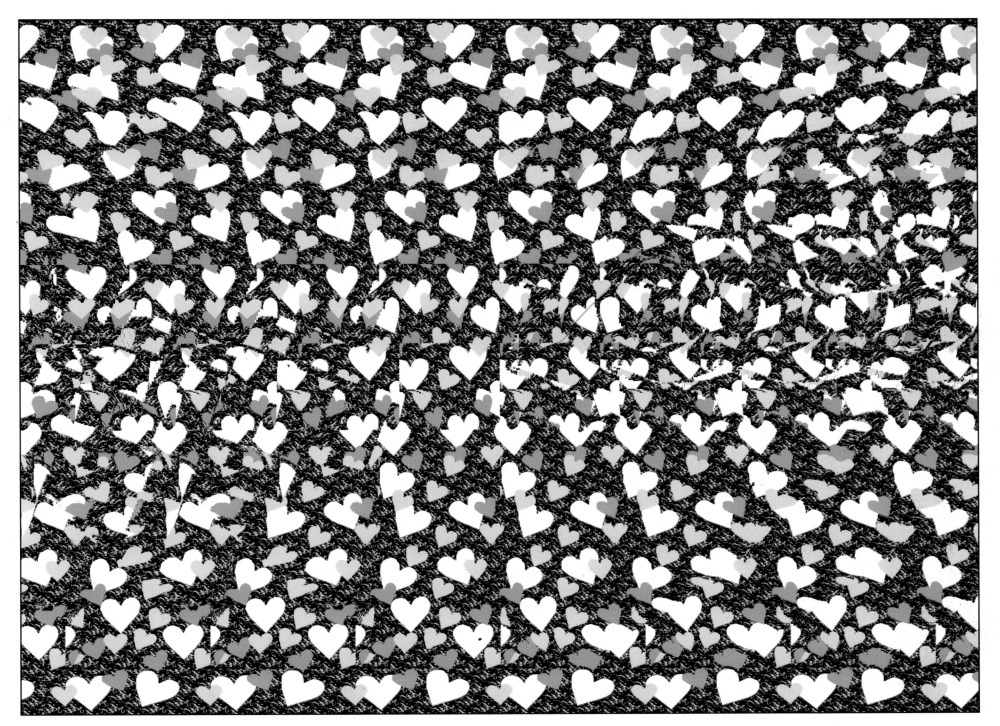

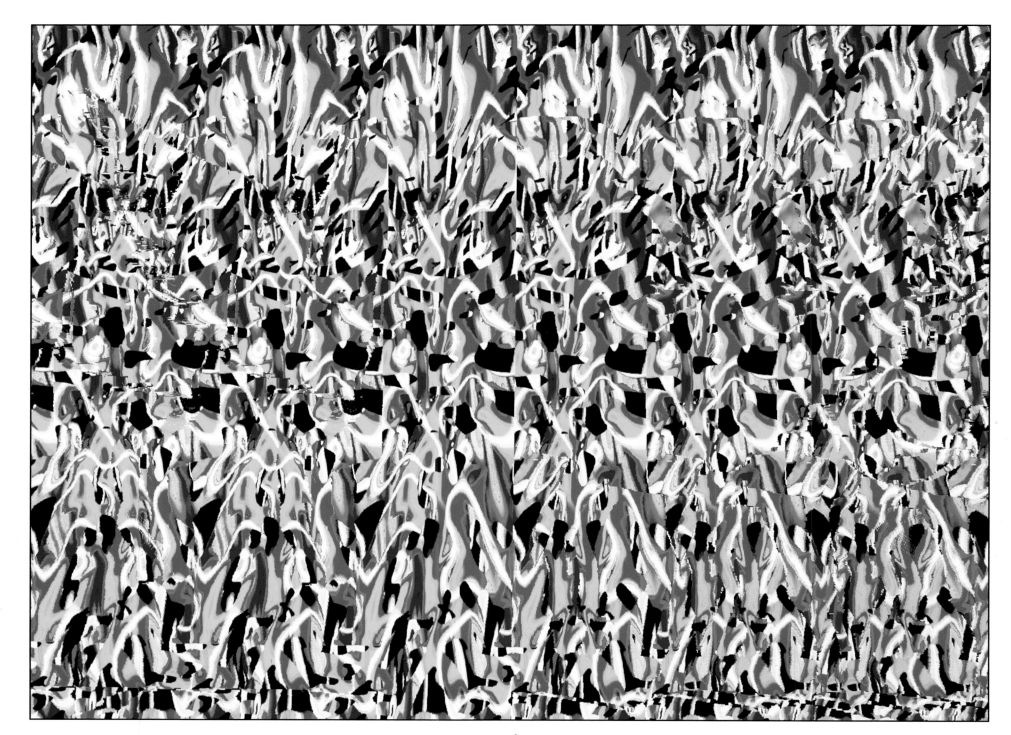

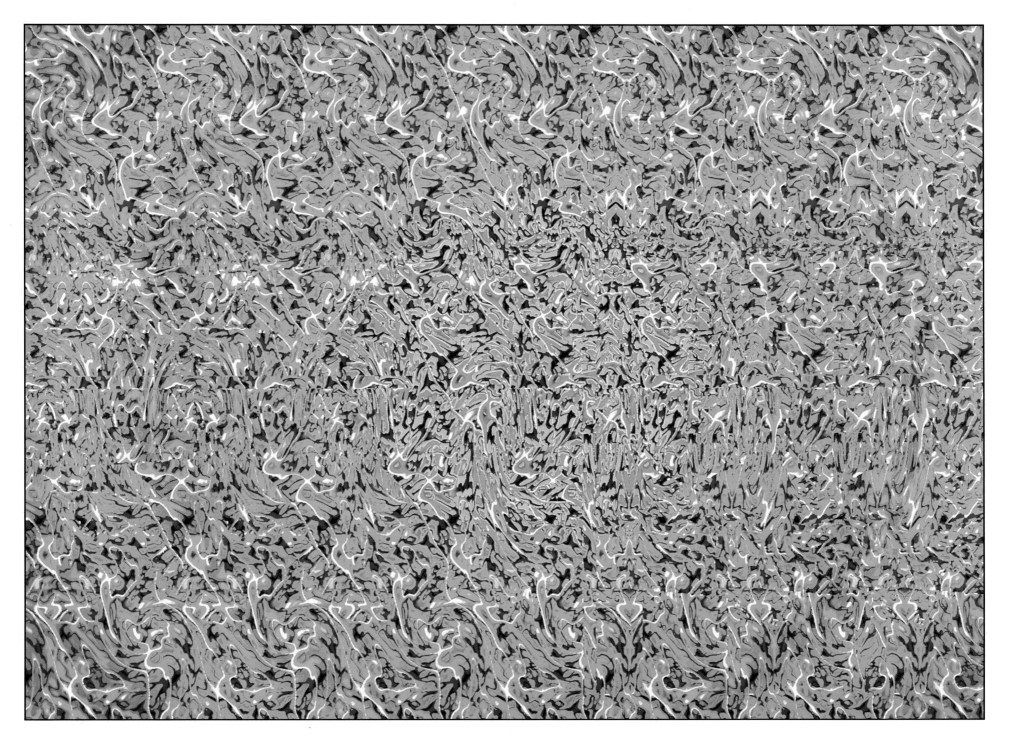

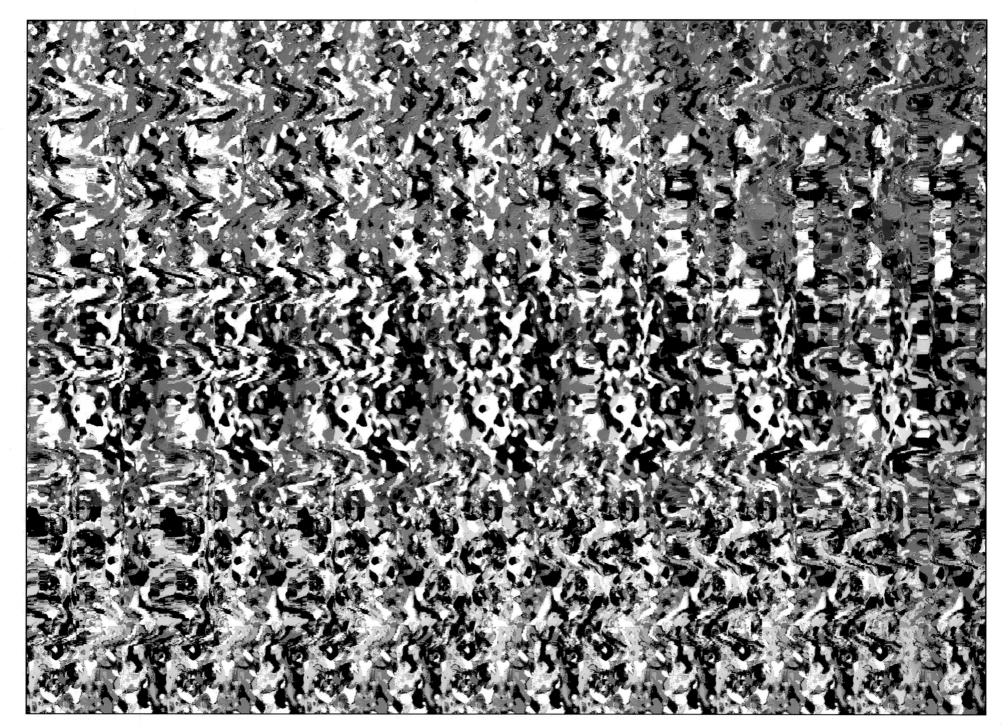

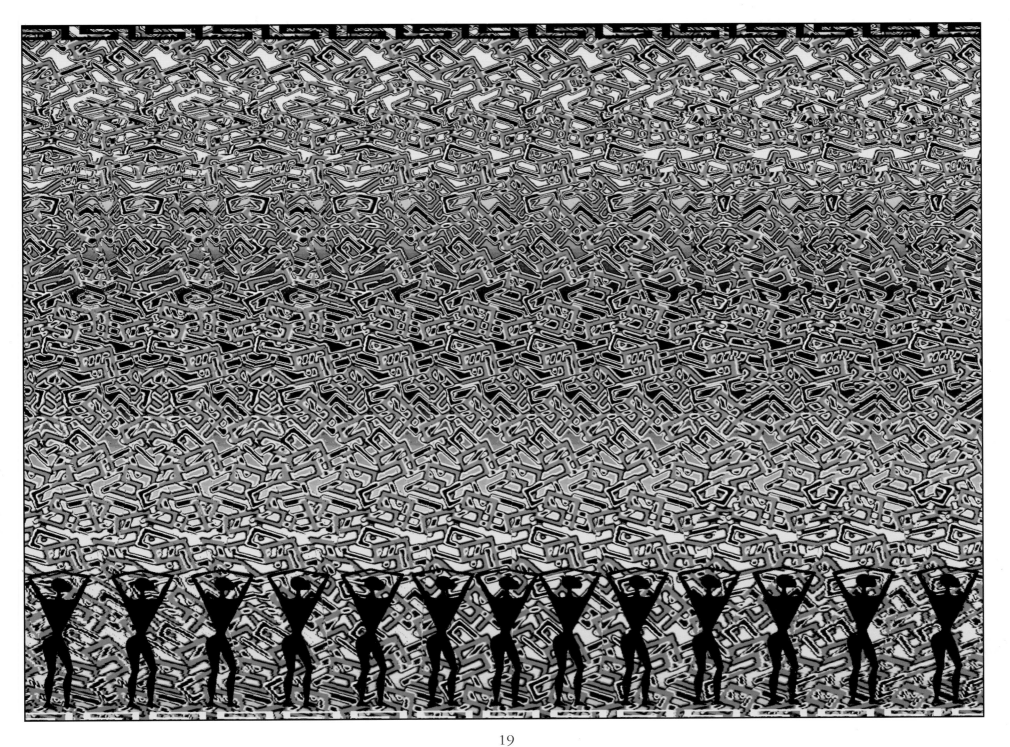

19

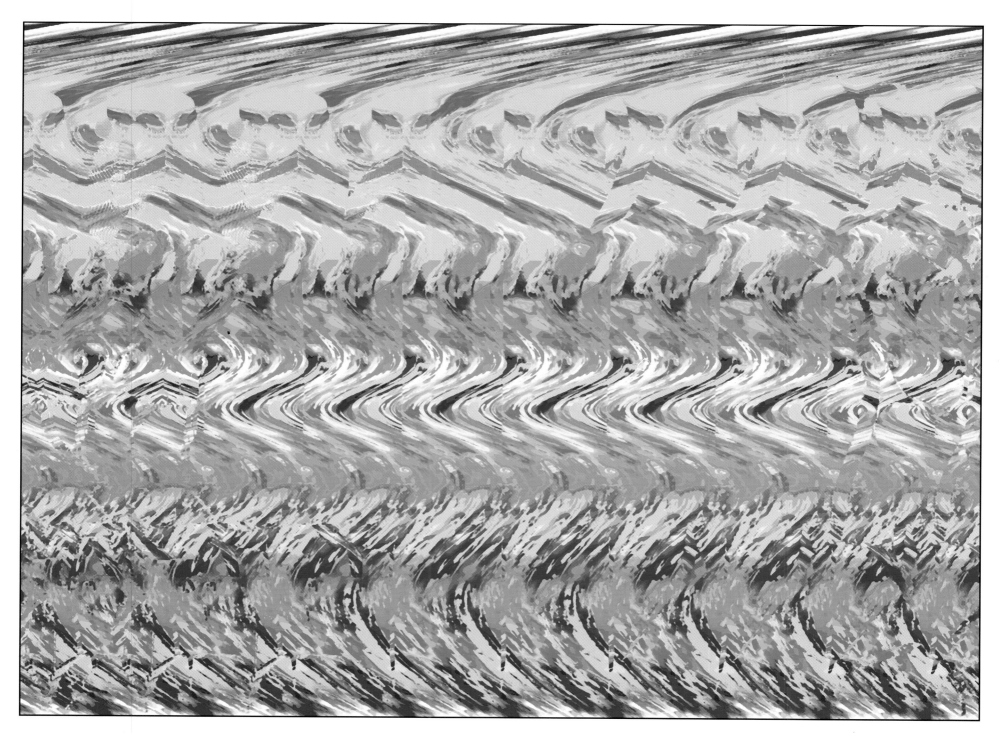

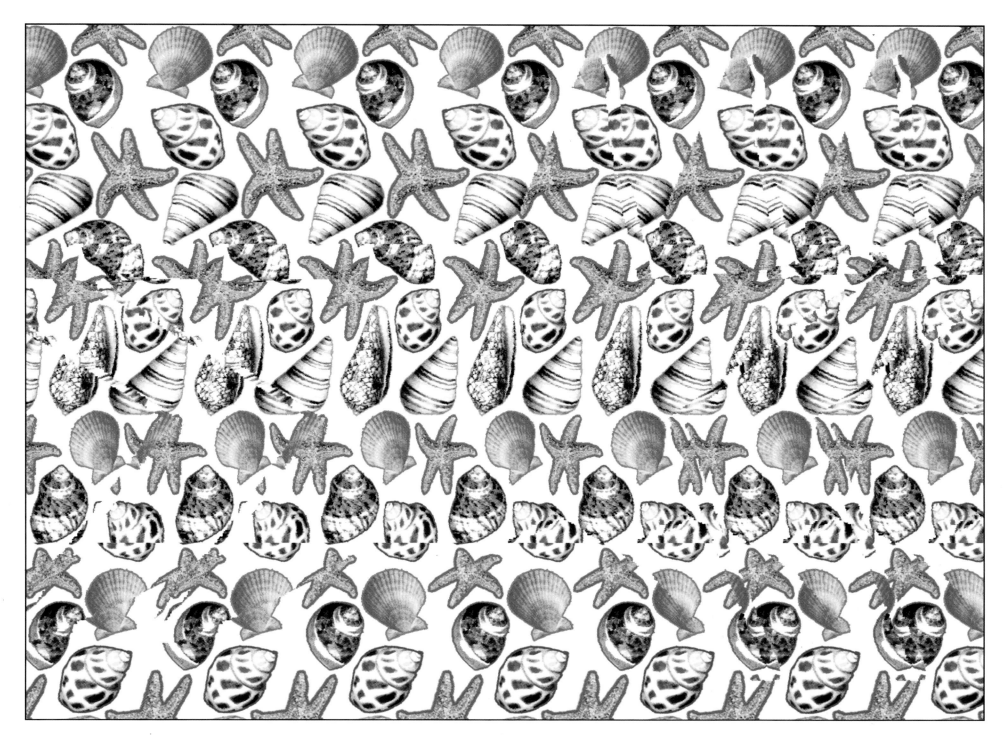

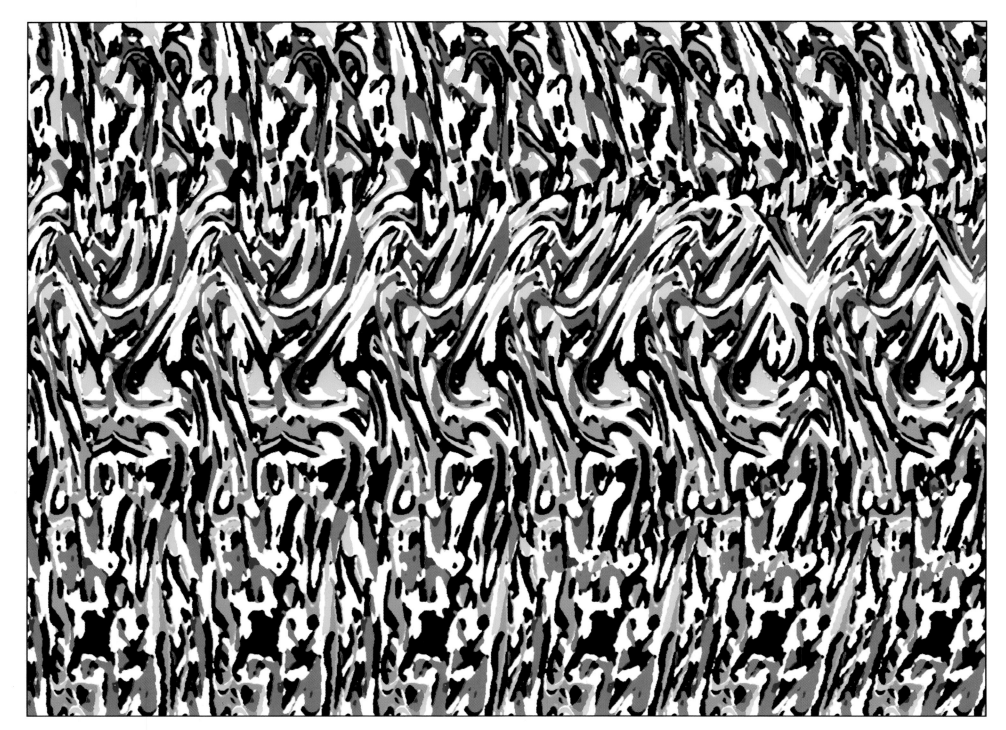

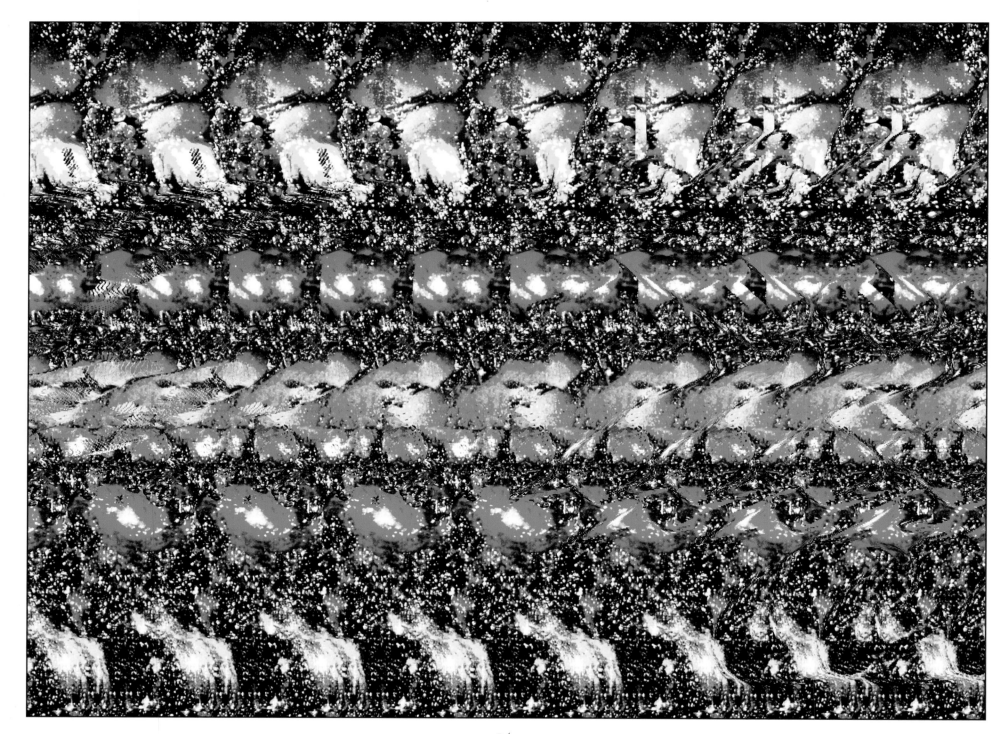

24

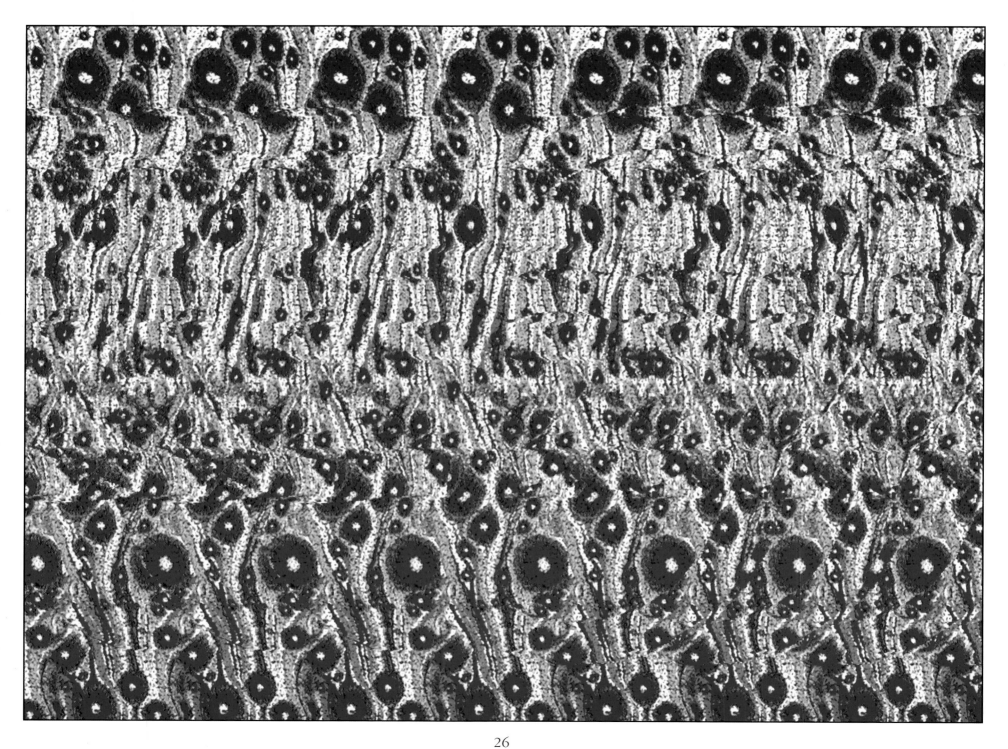

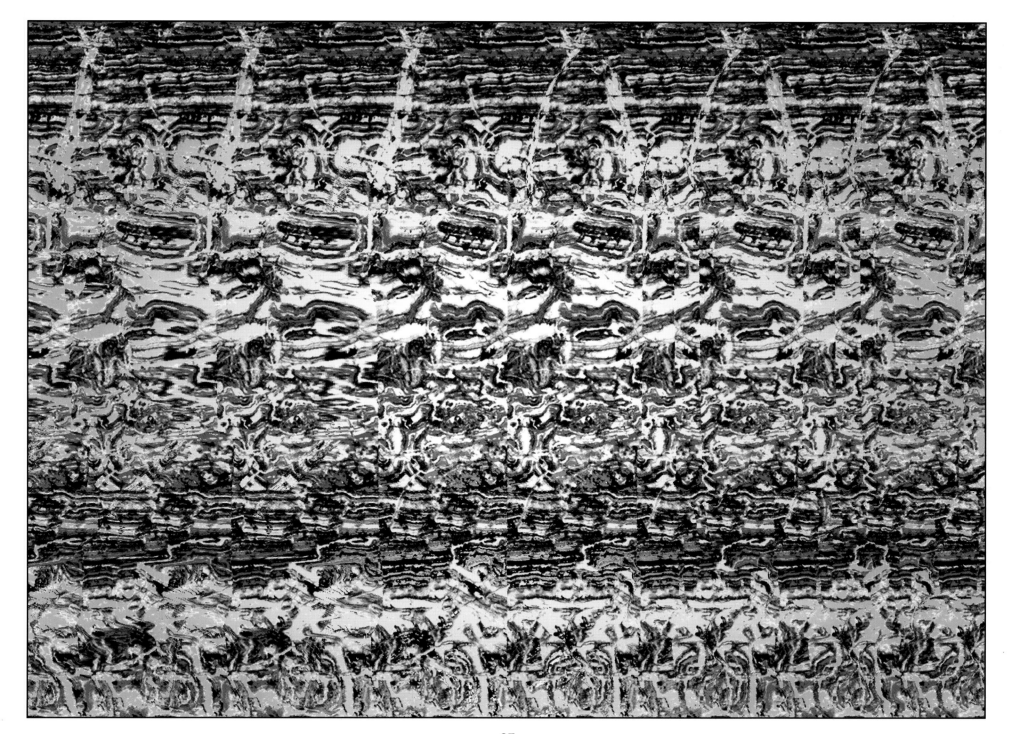

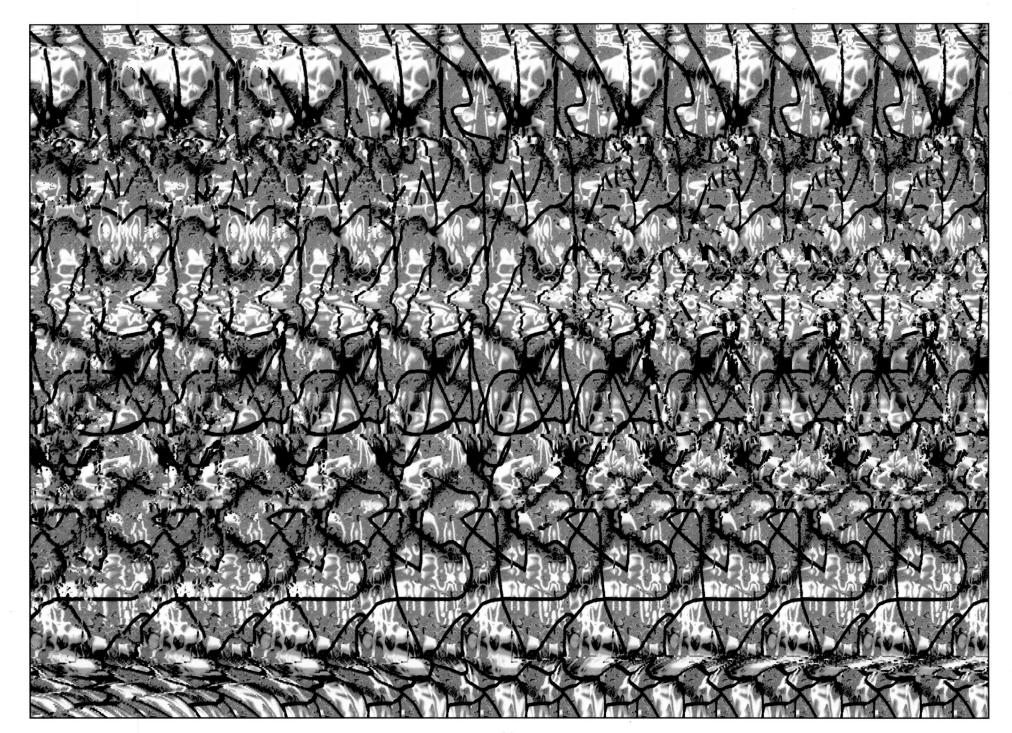

28

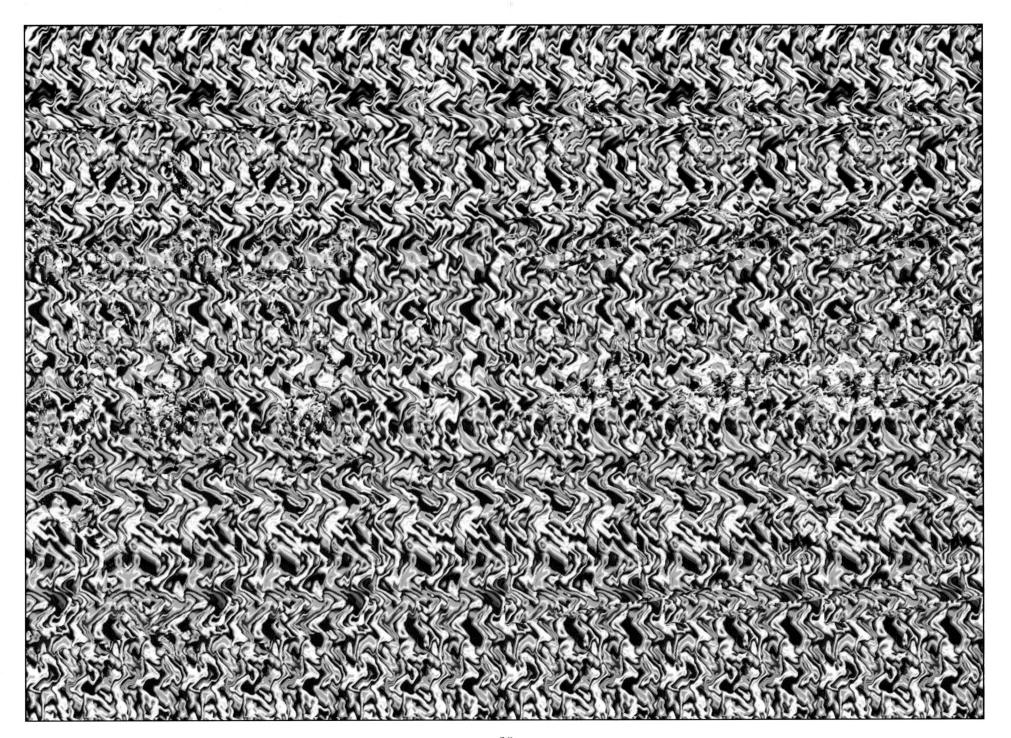

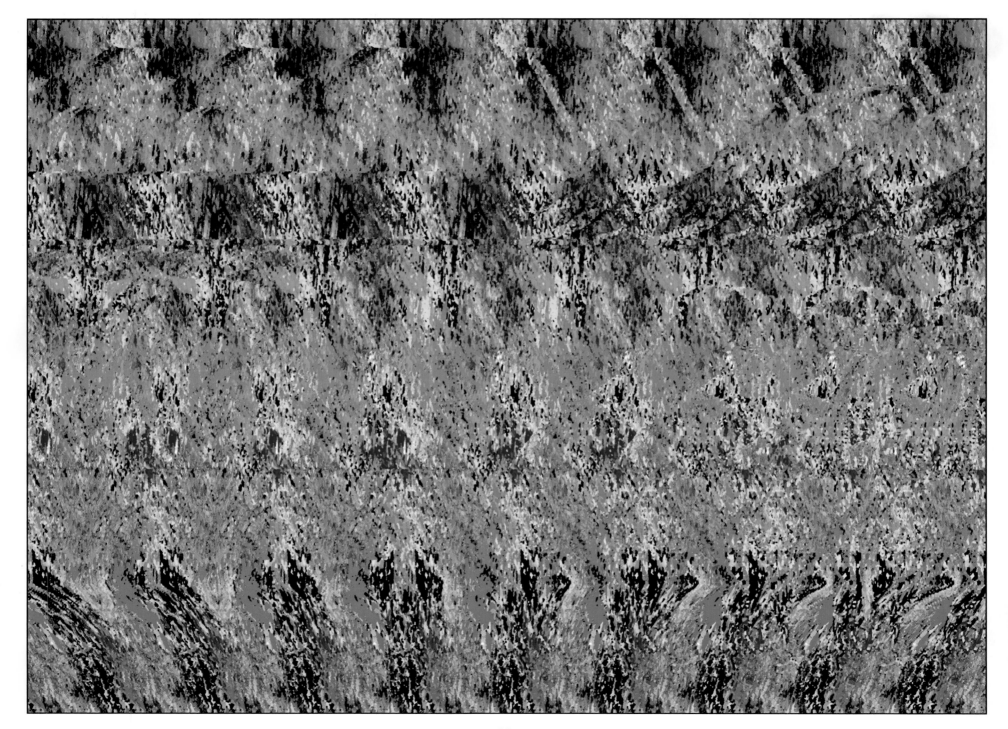

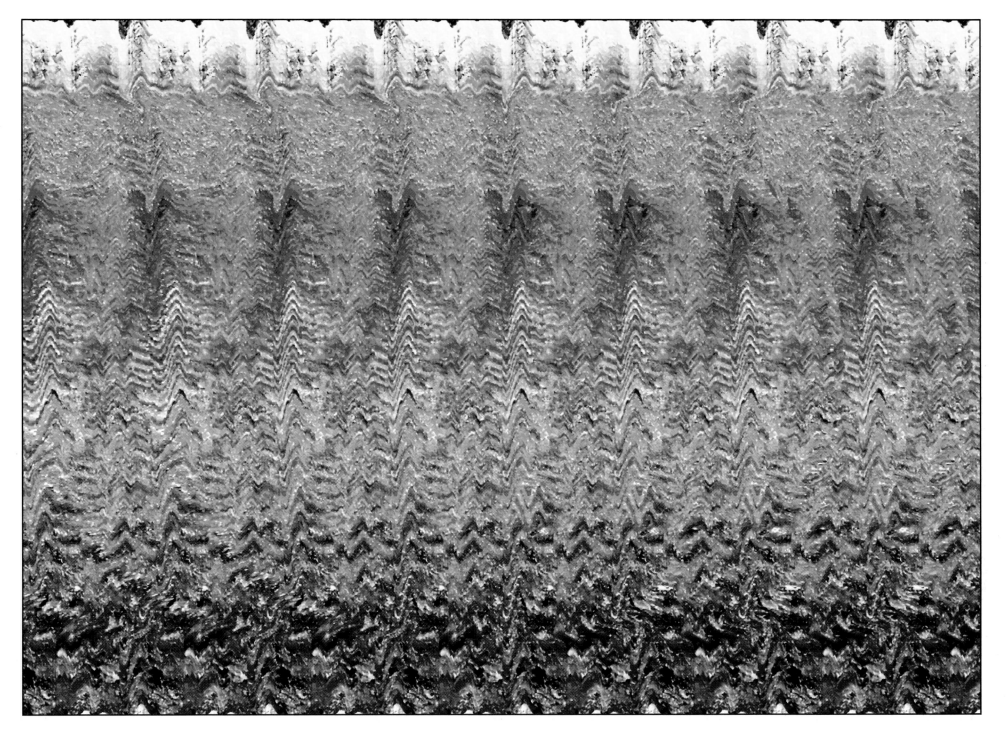

31

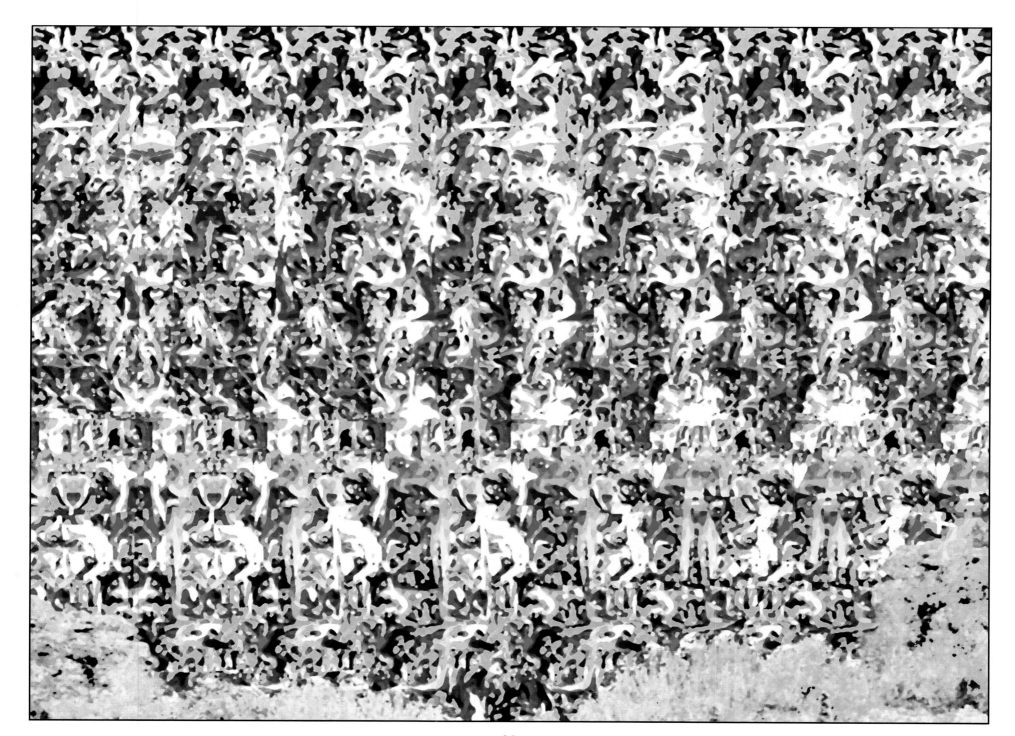

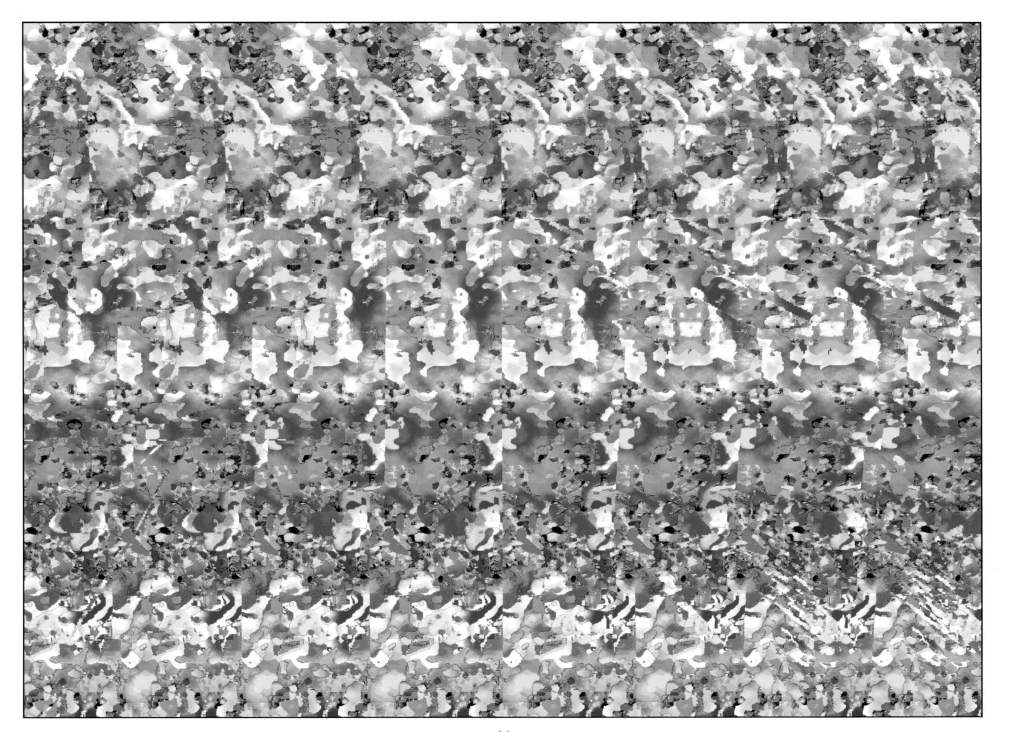

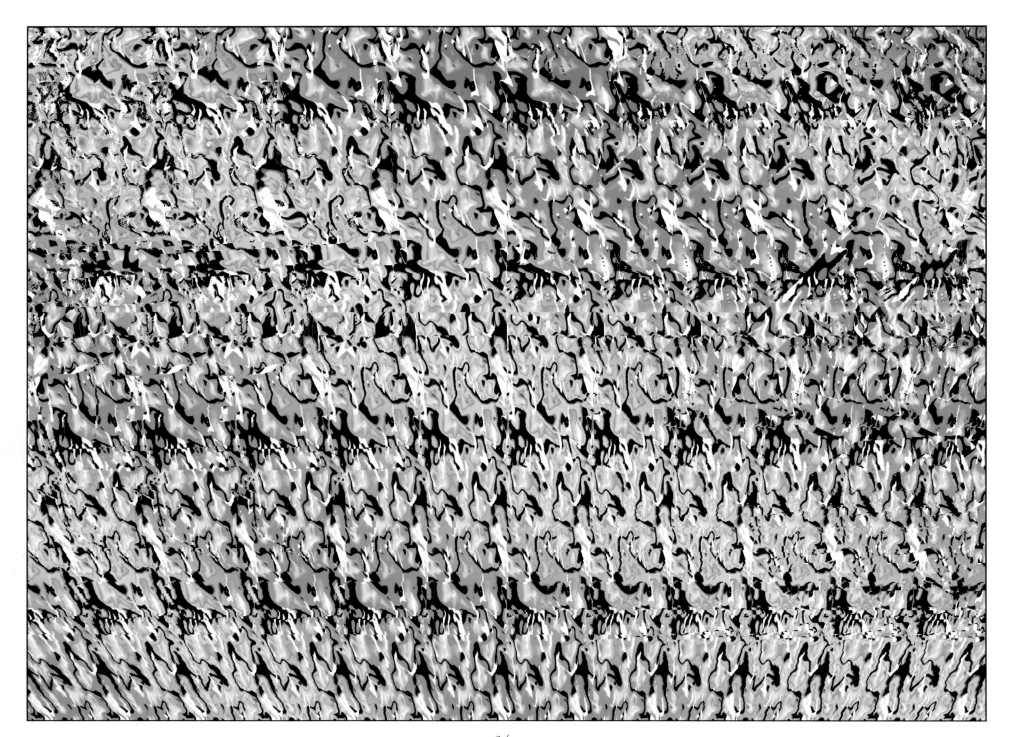

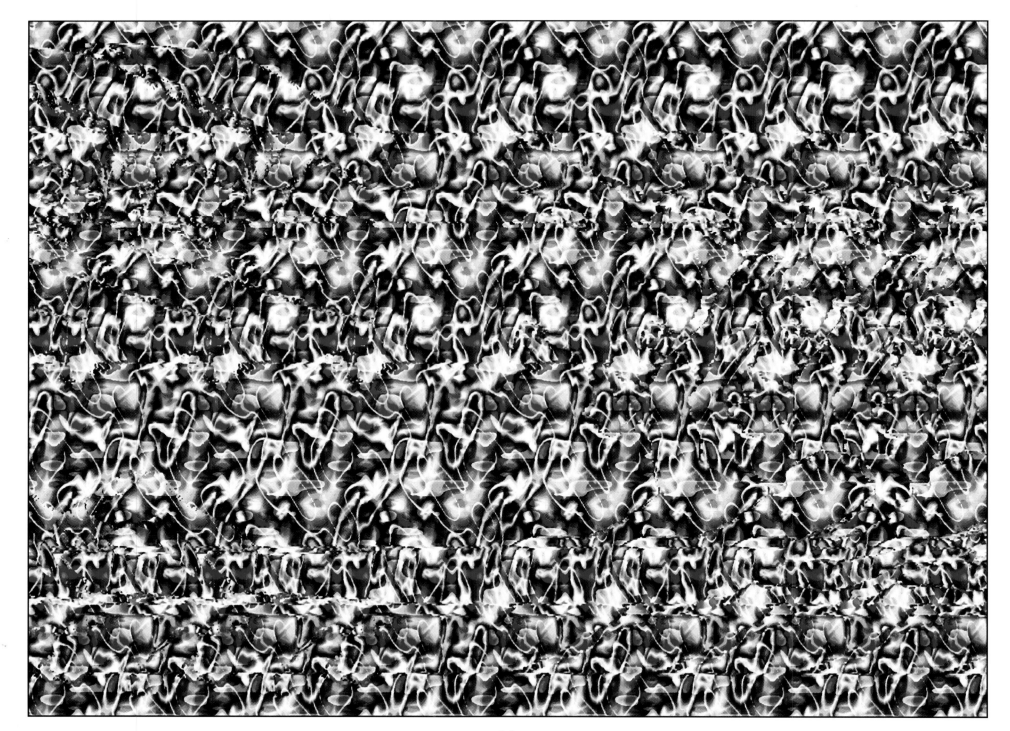

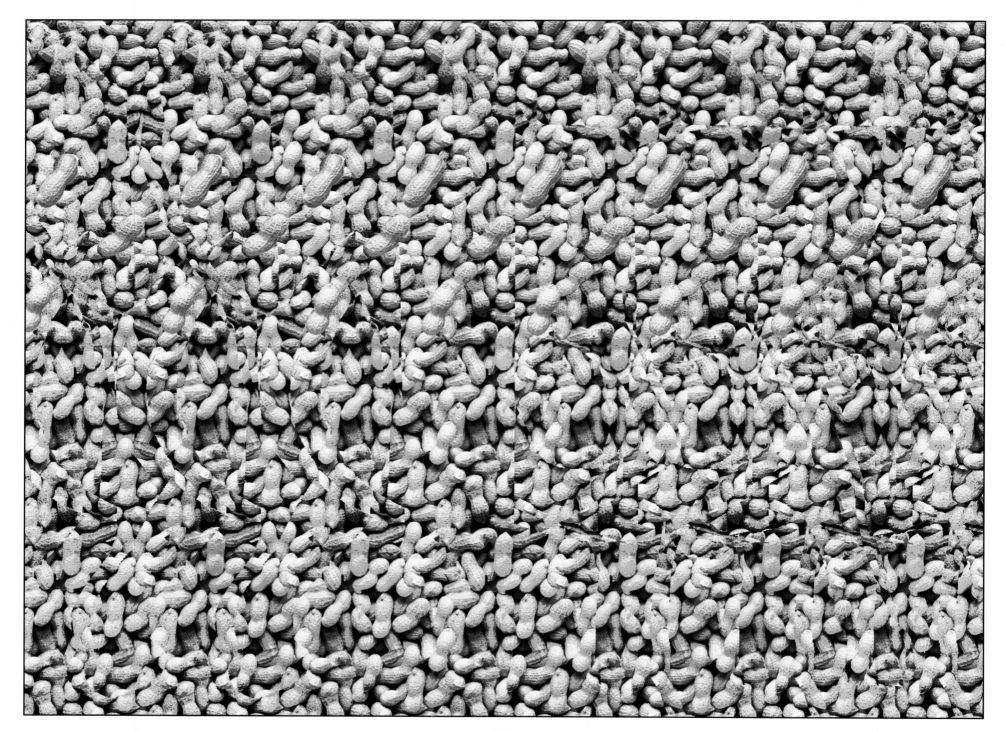

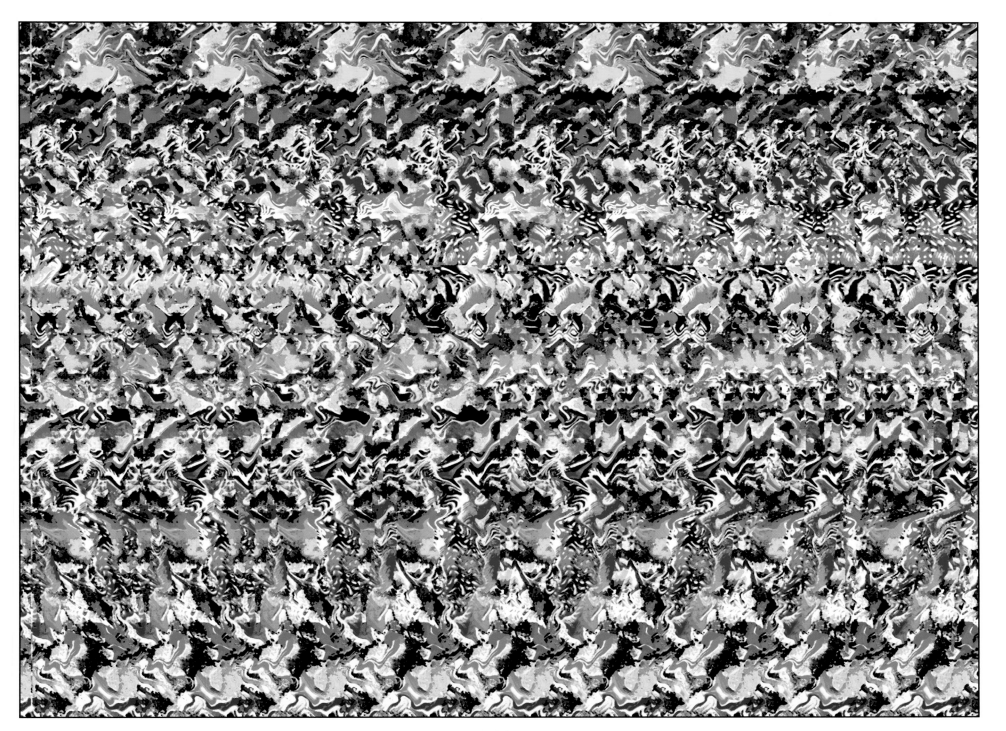

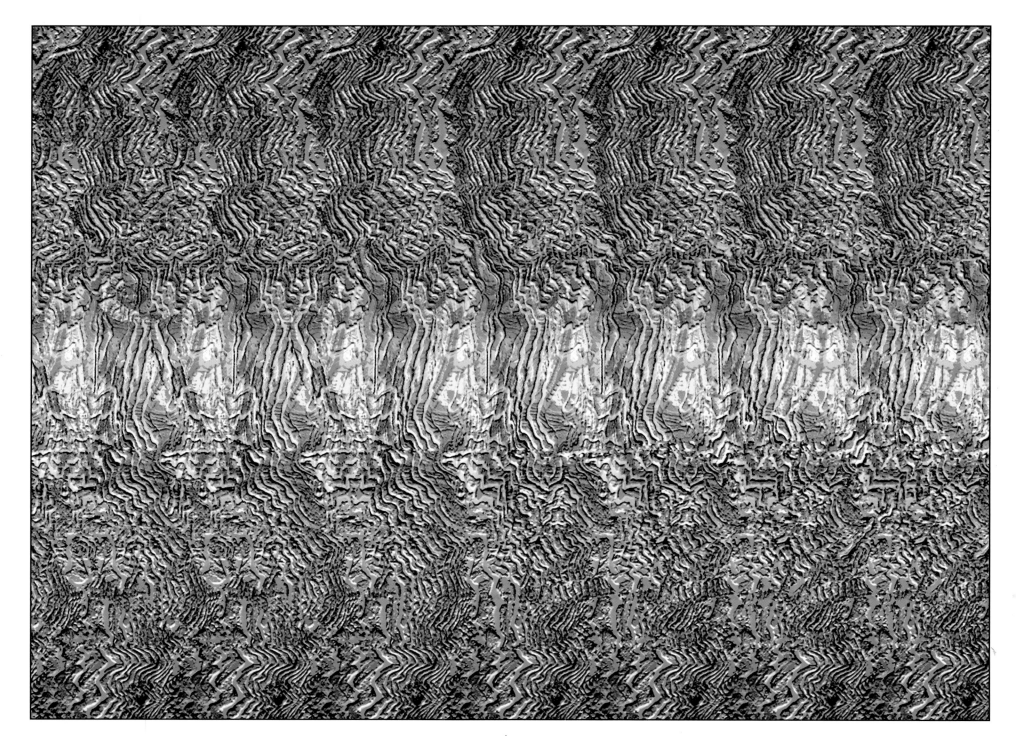

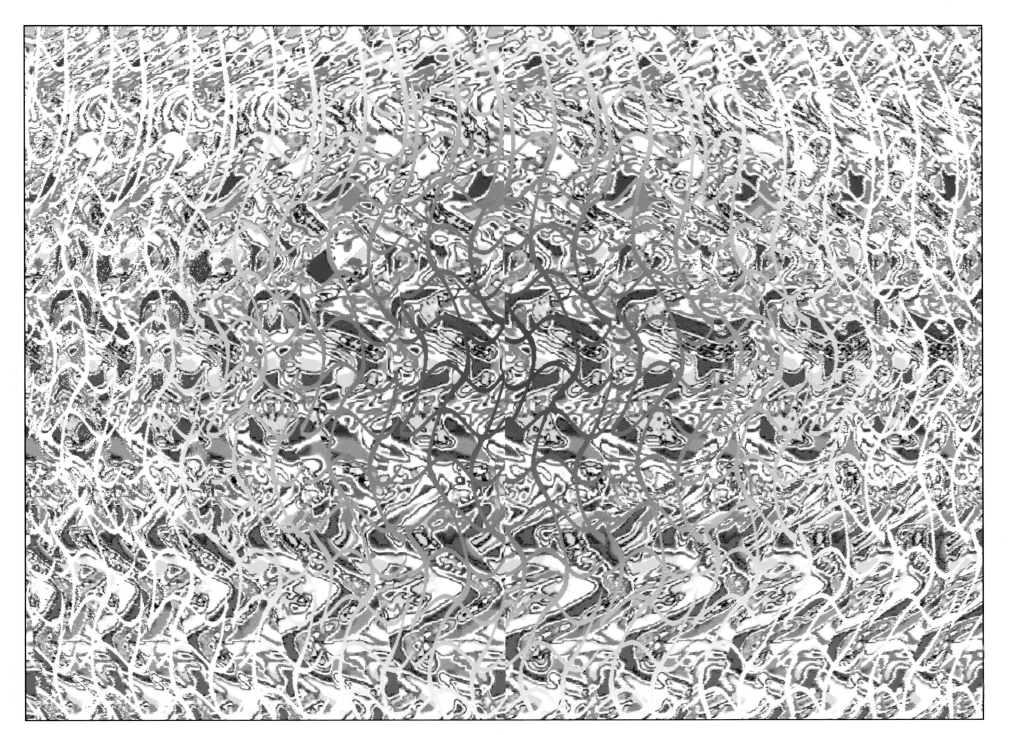

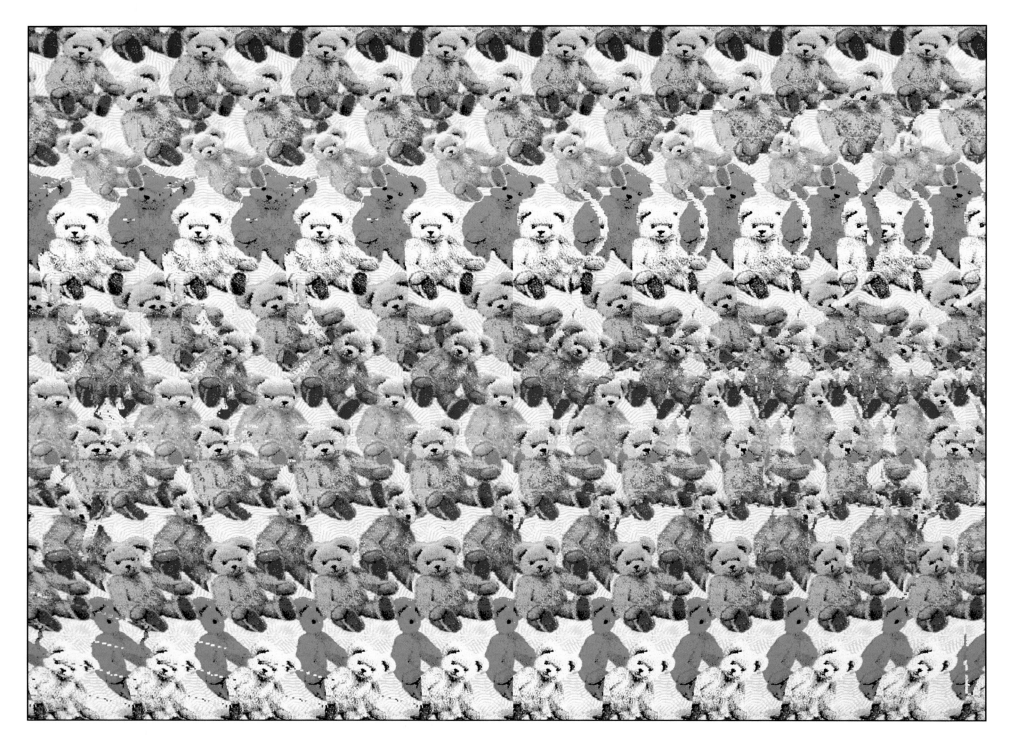

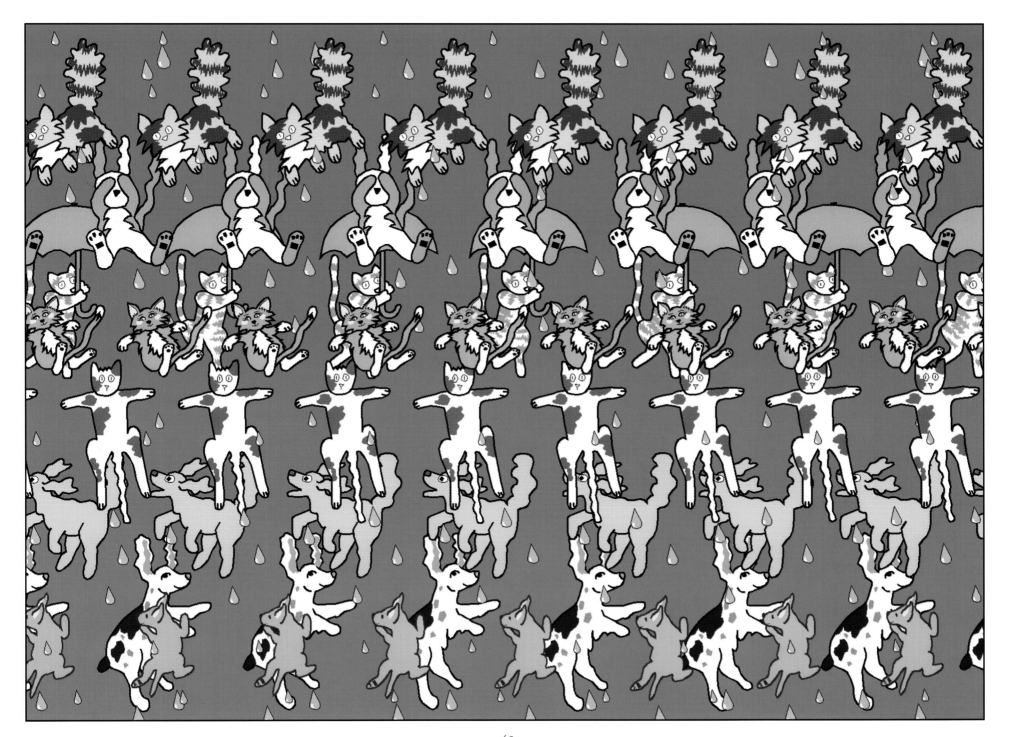

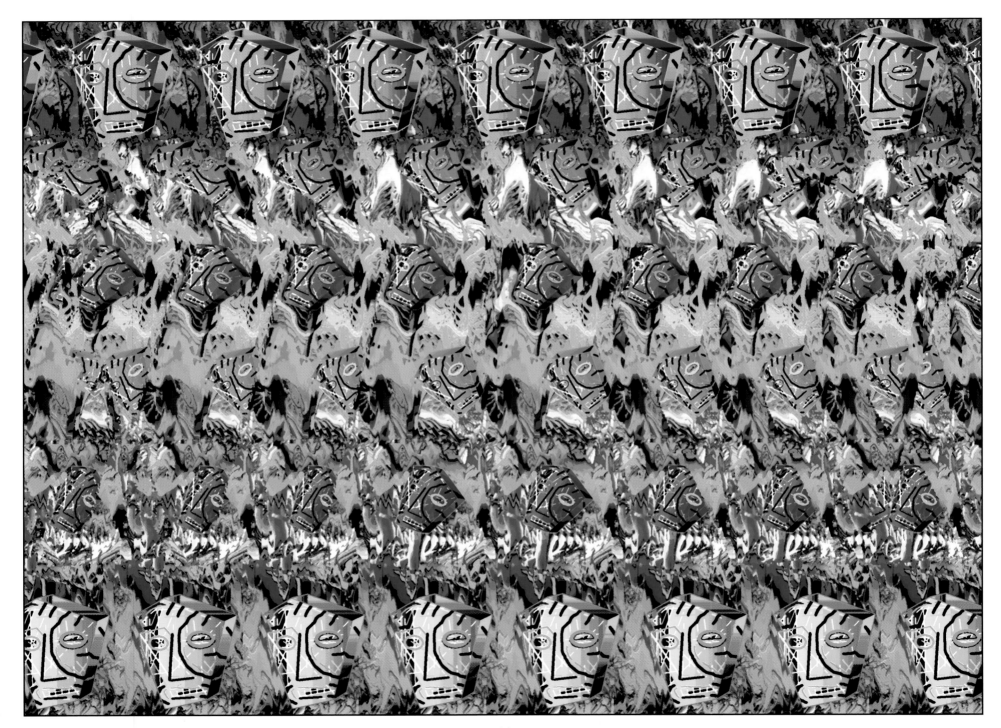

44

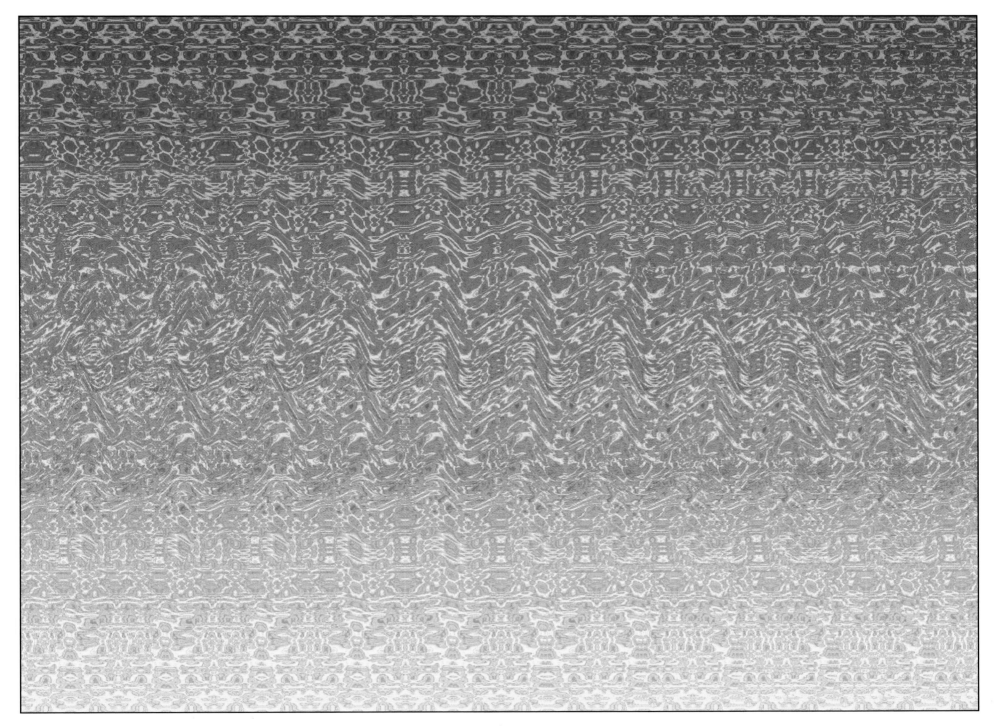

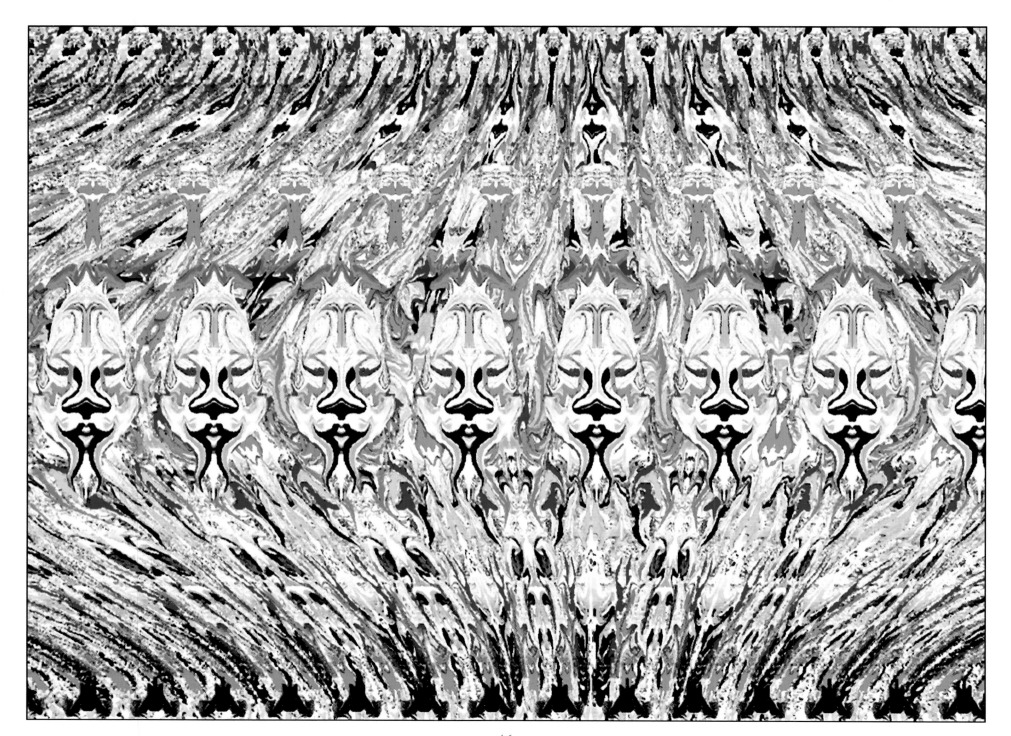

46

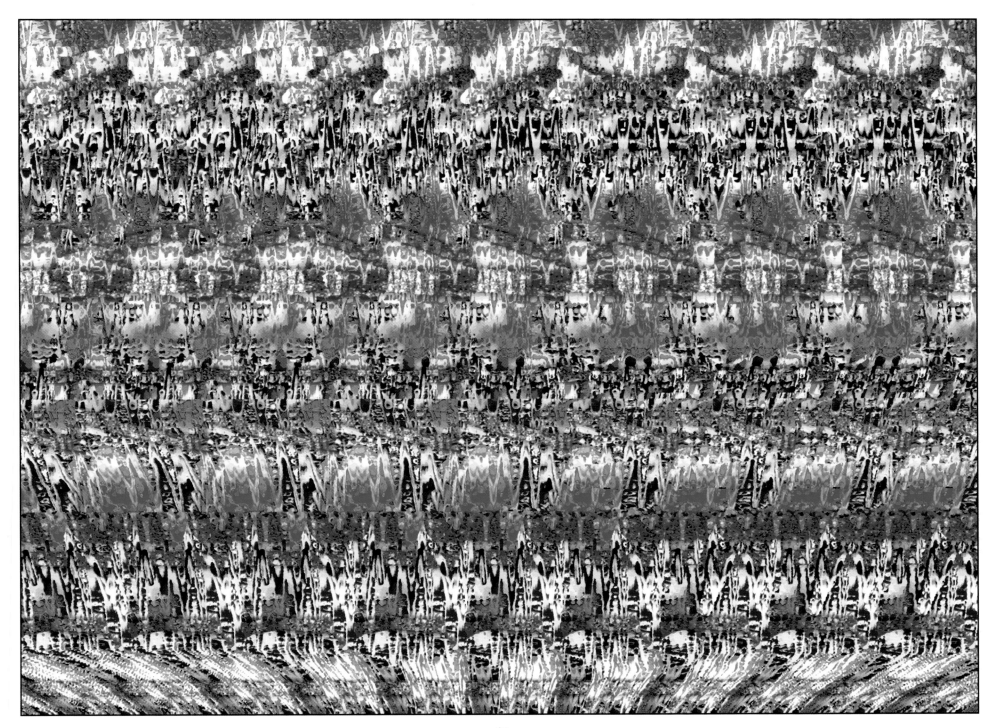

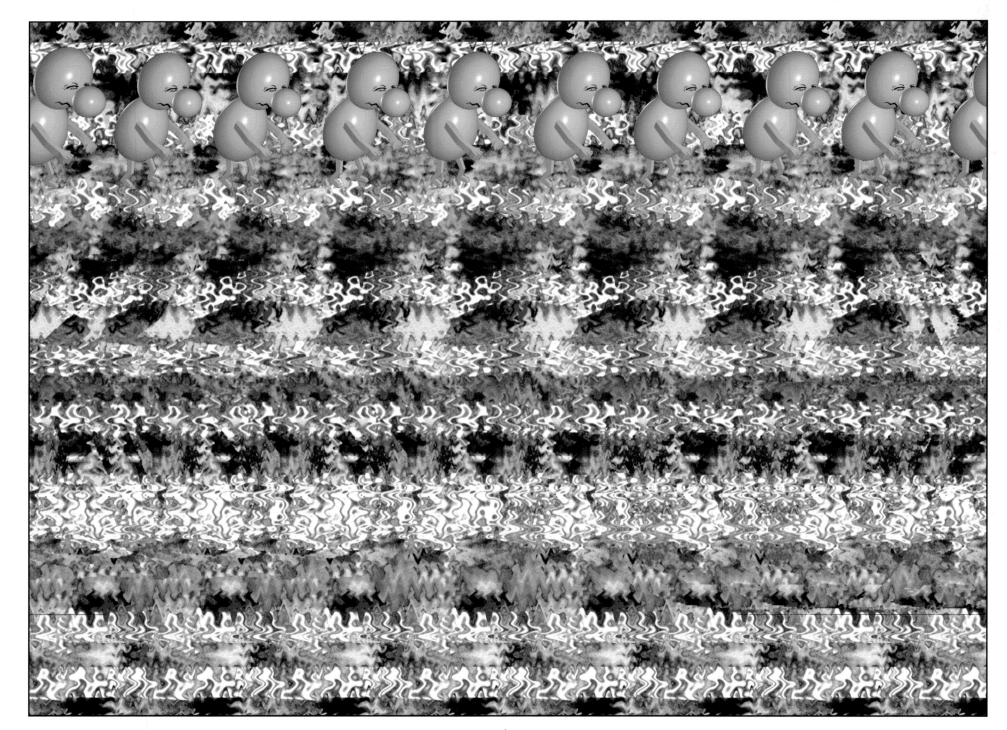

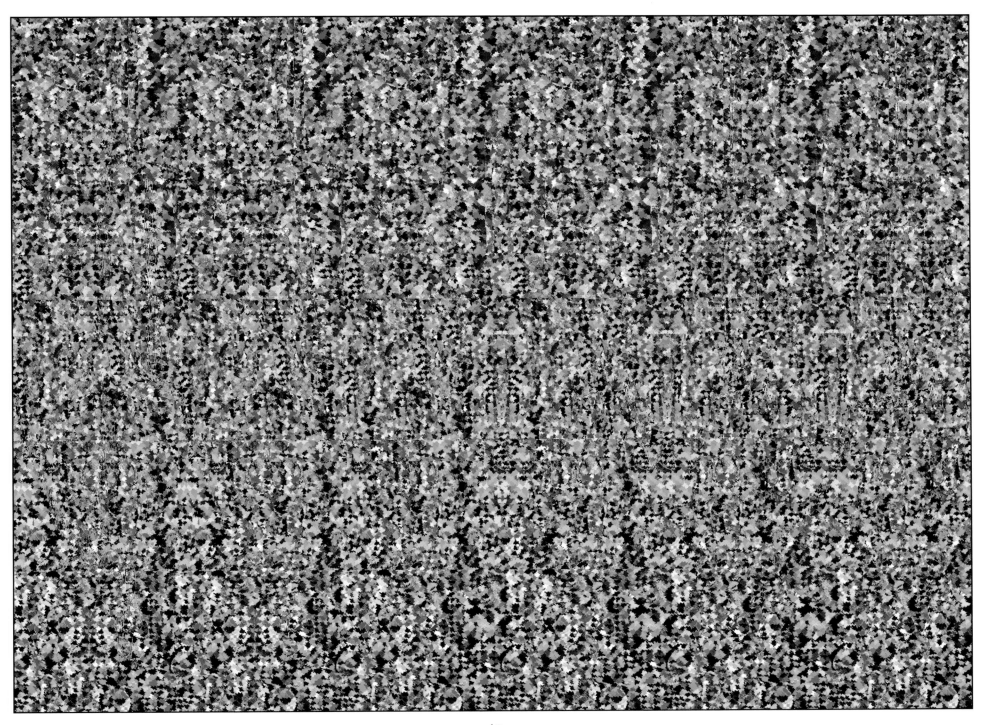

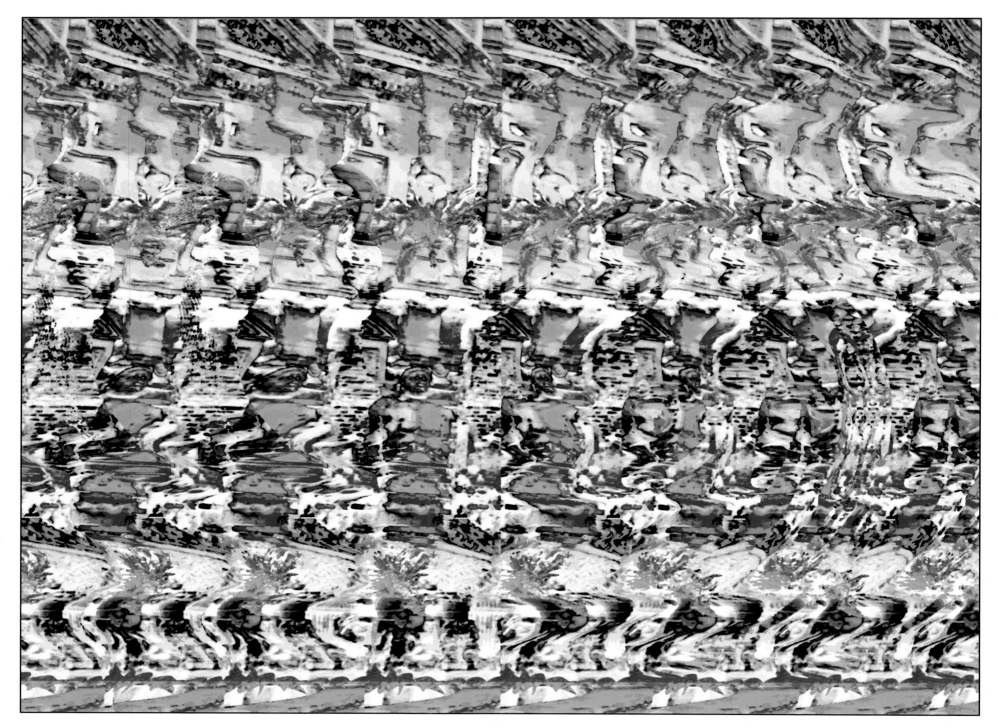

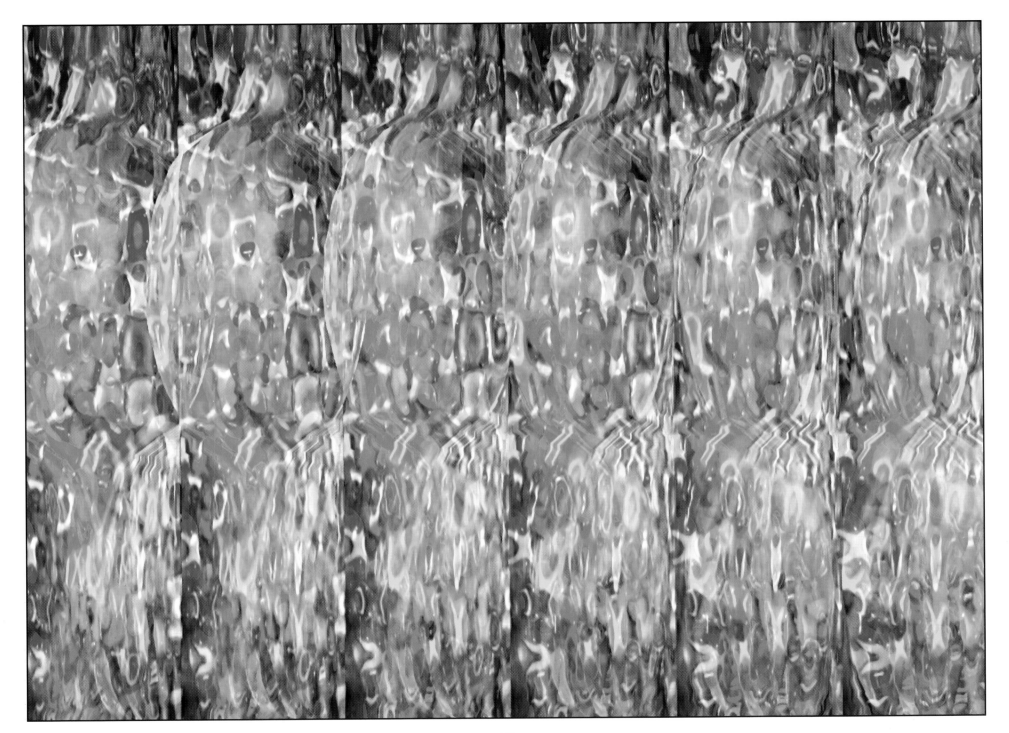

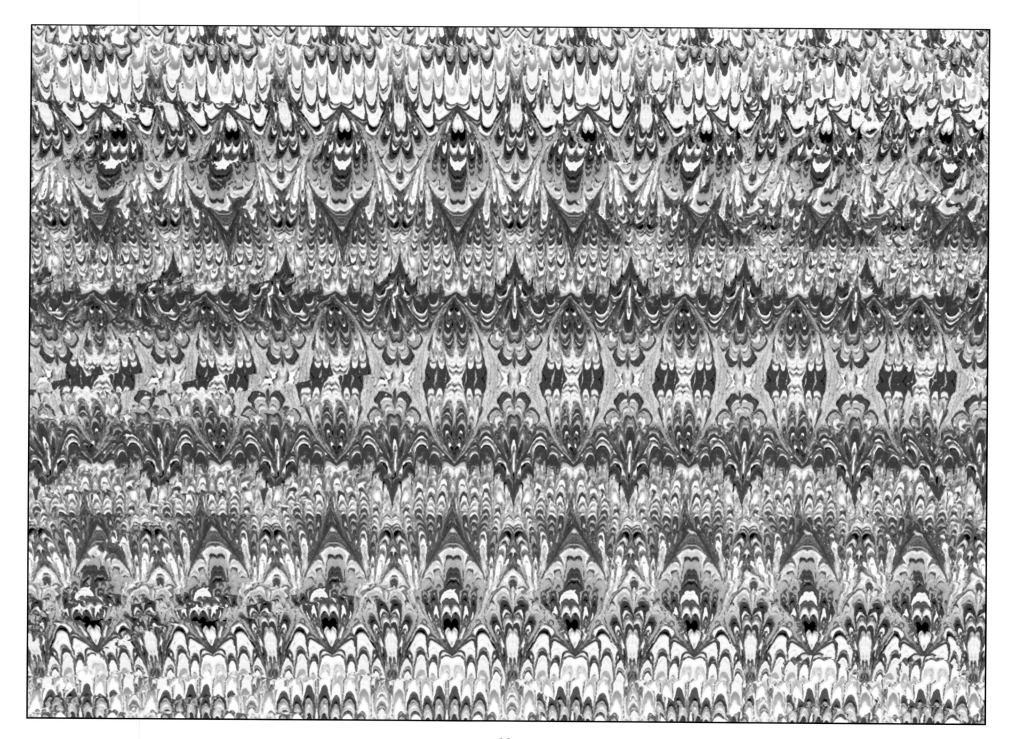

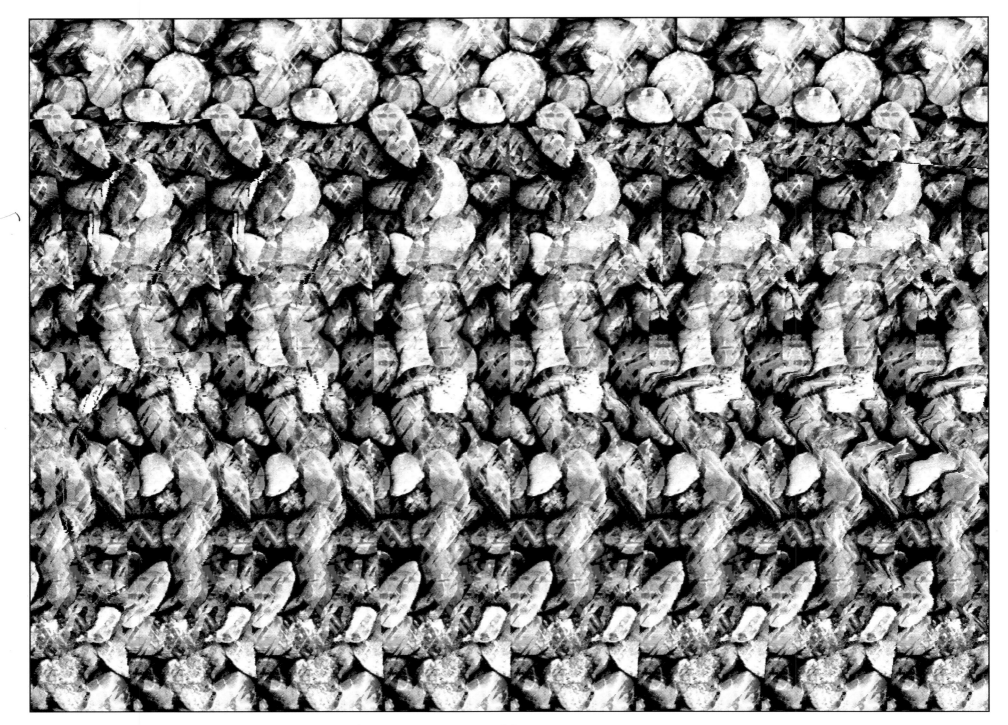

54

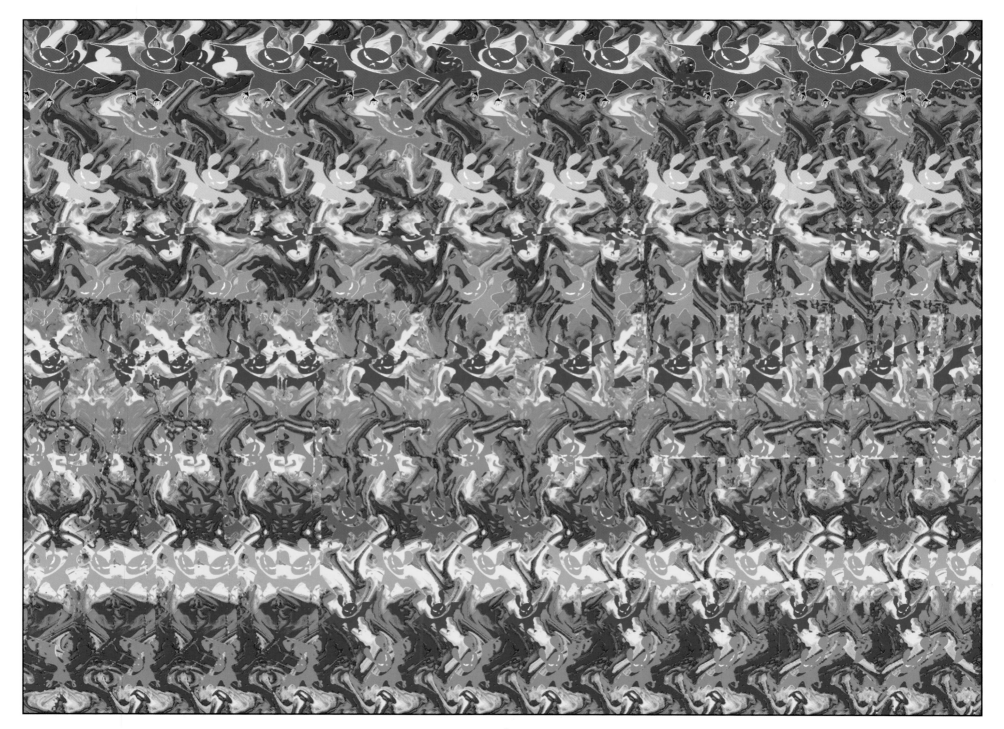

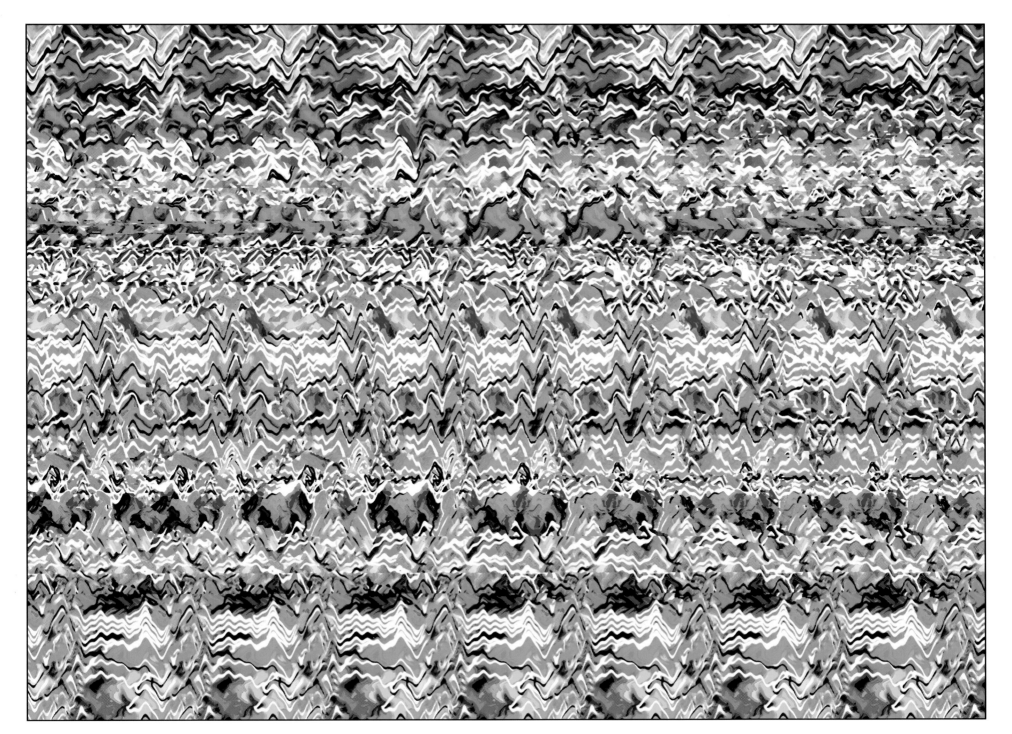

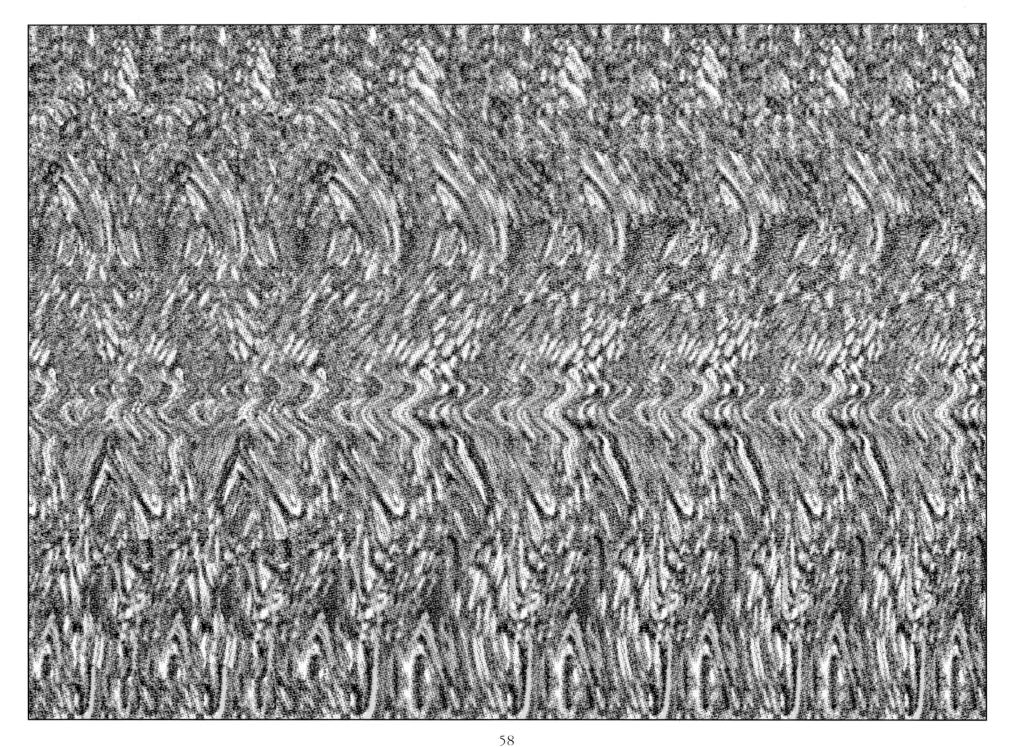

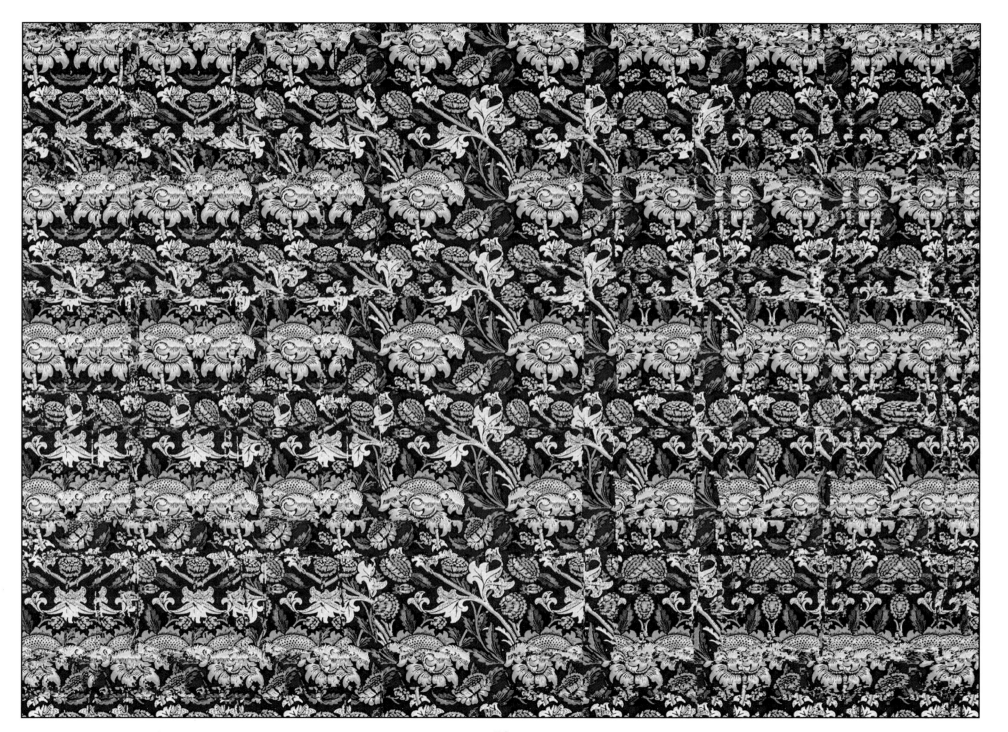

59

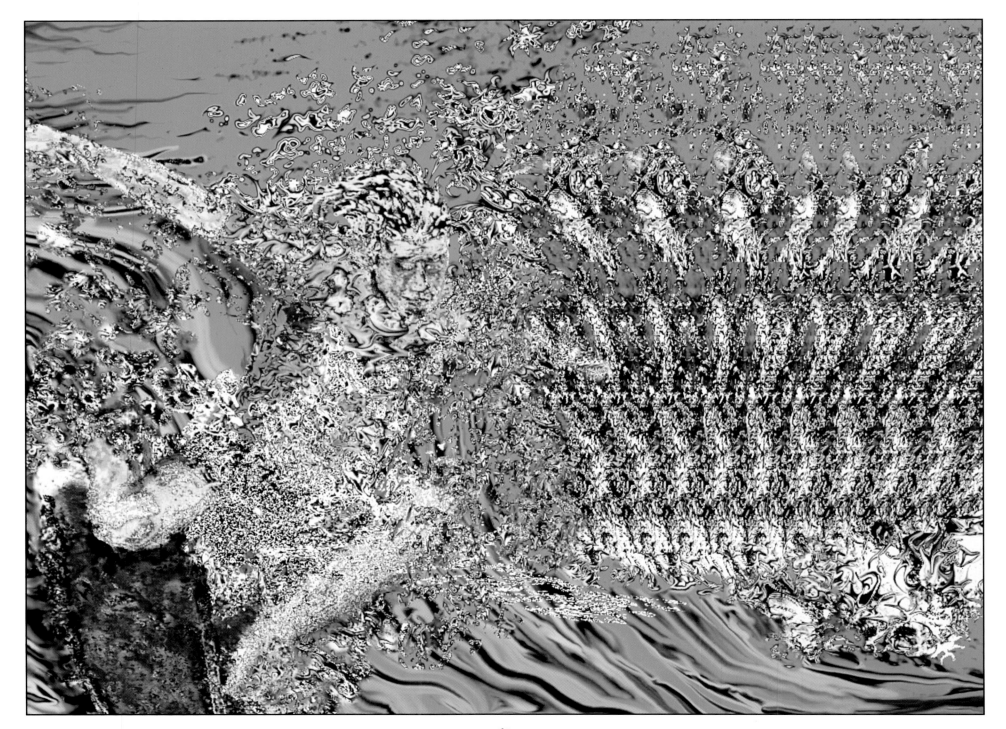

60

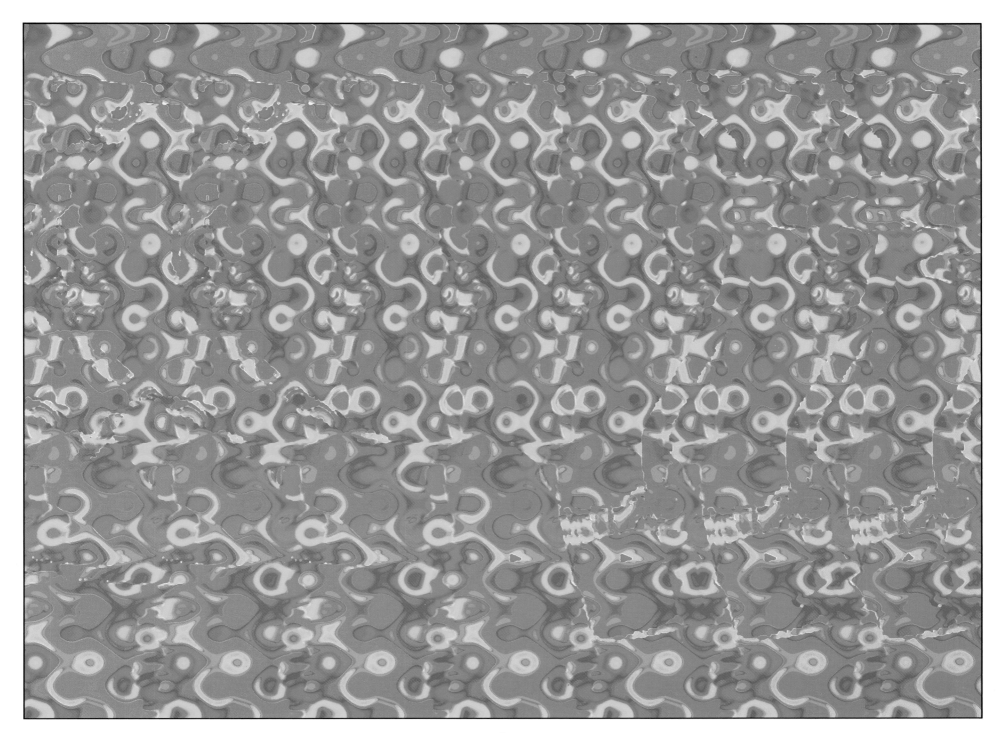

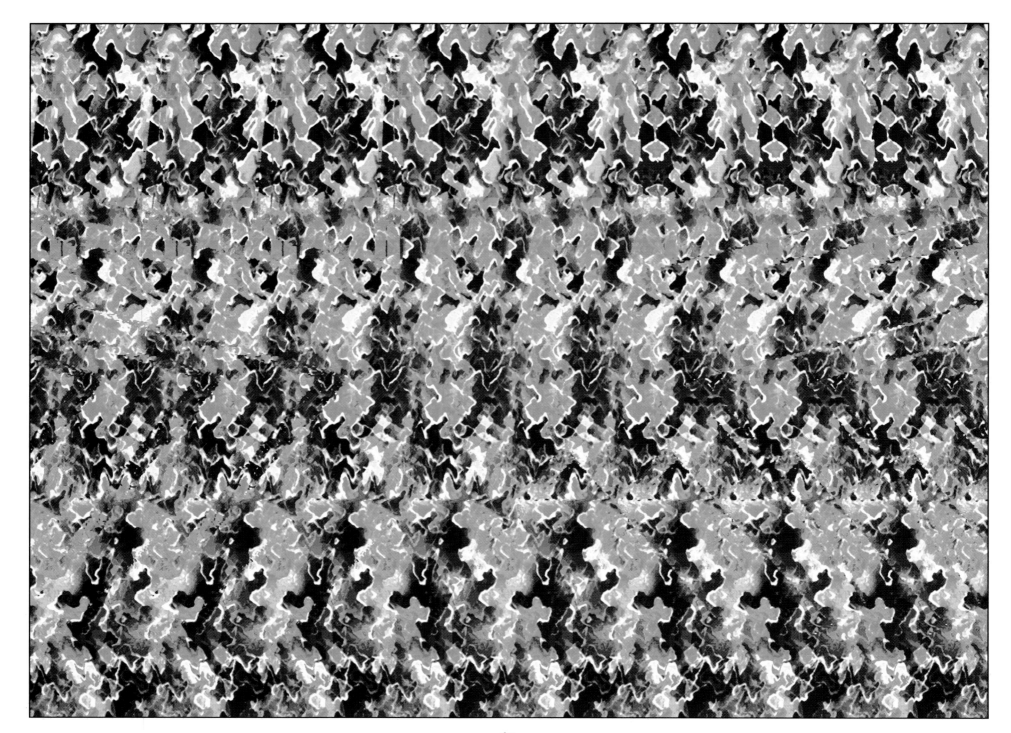

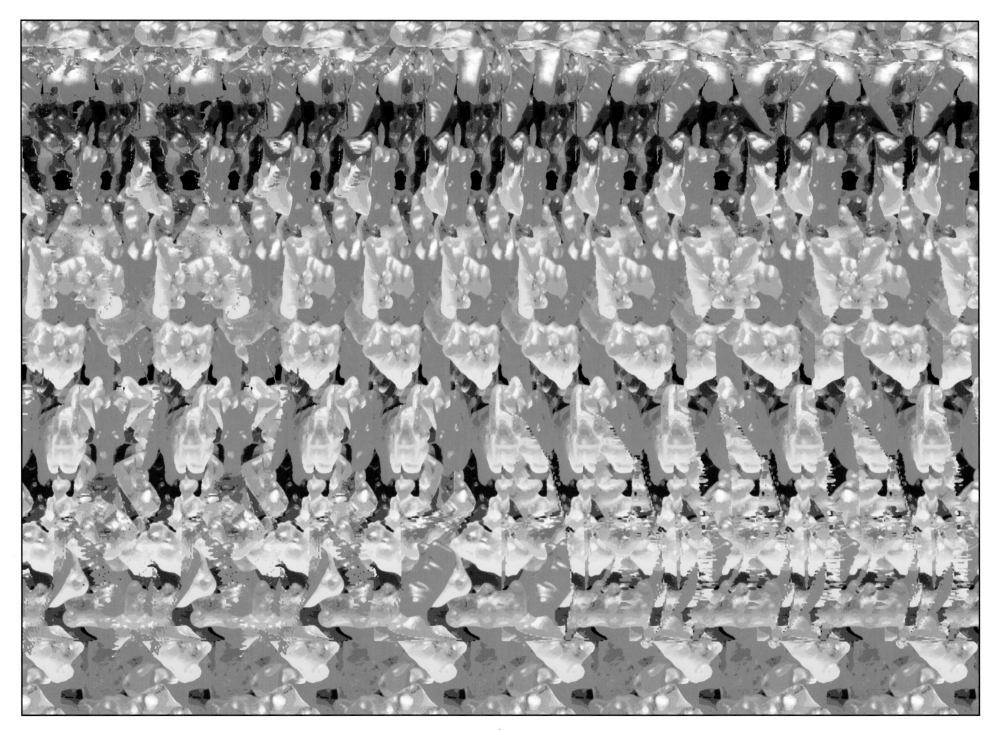

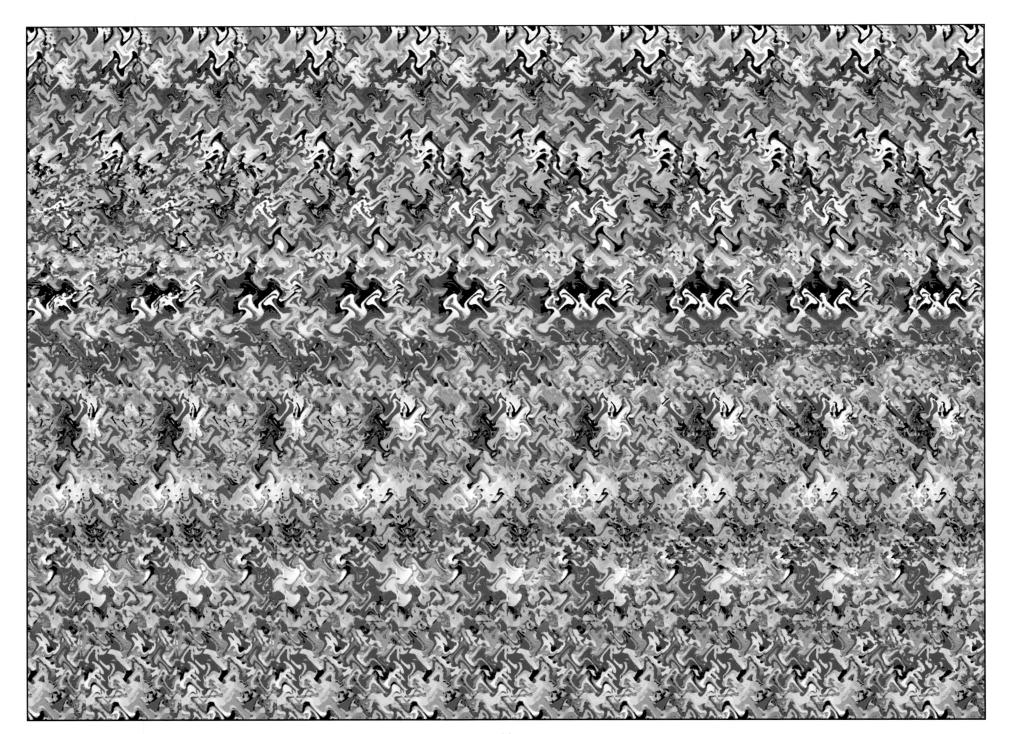

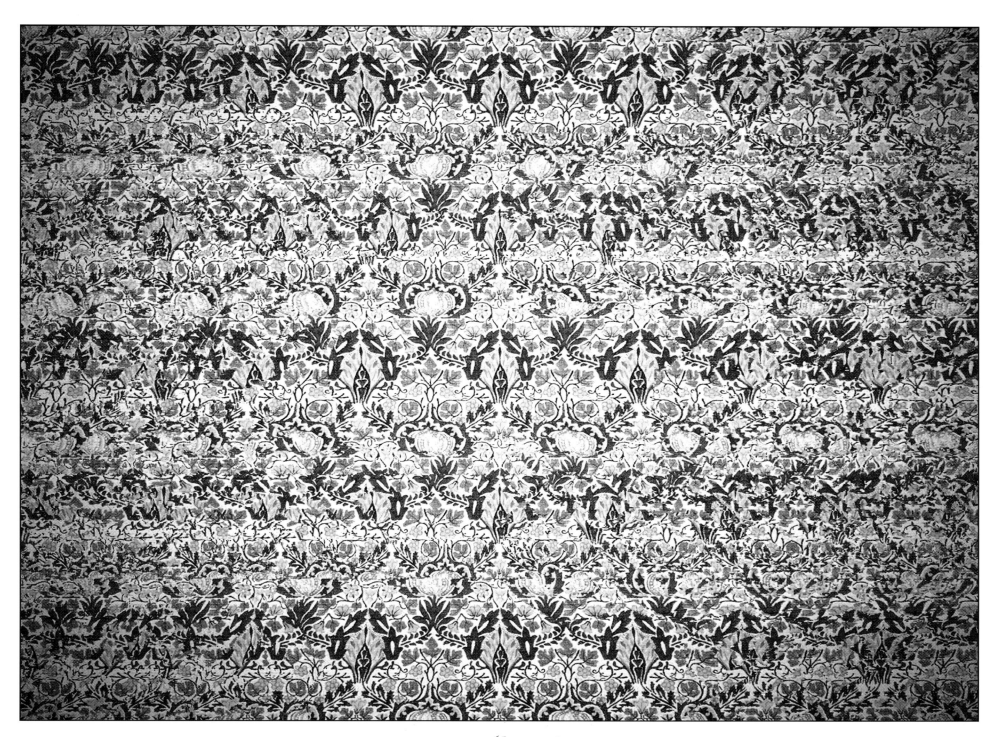

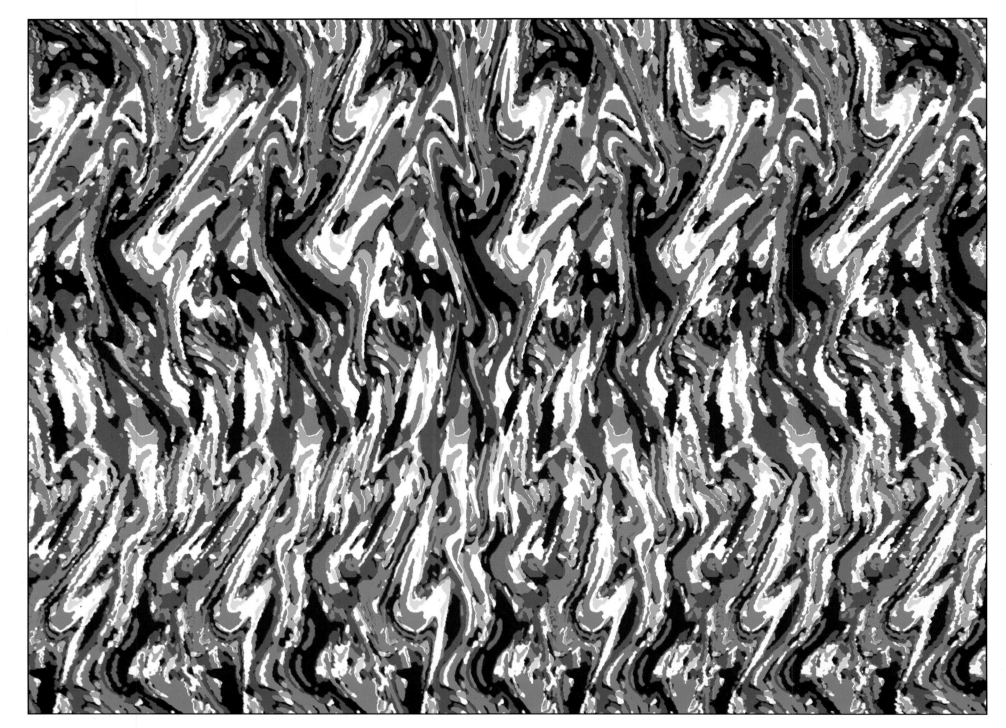

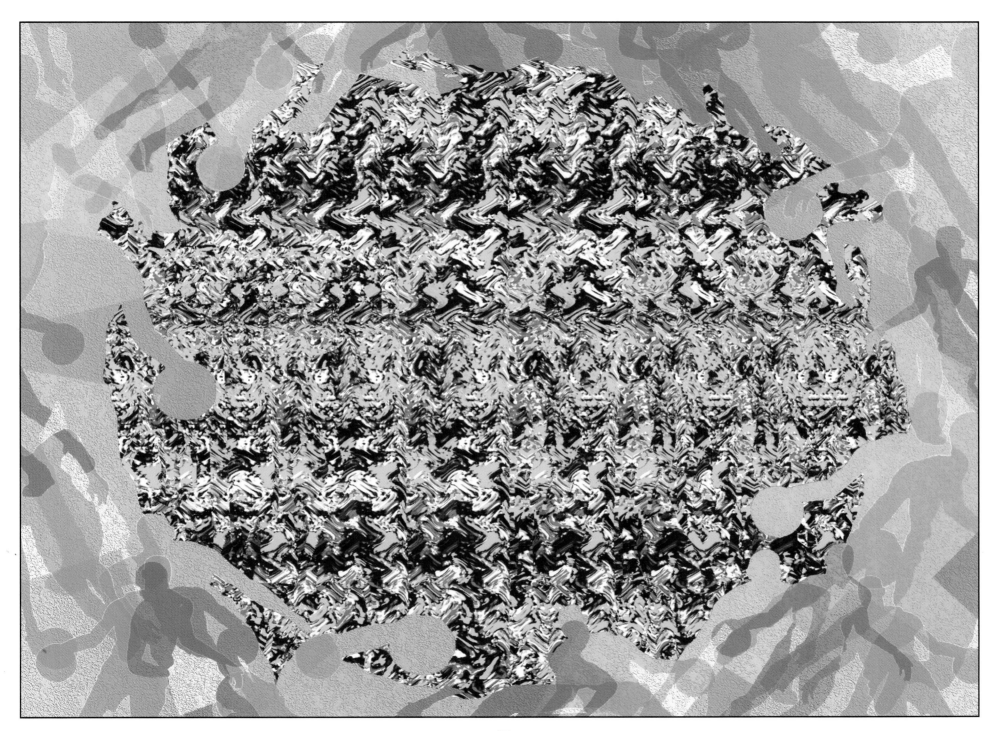

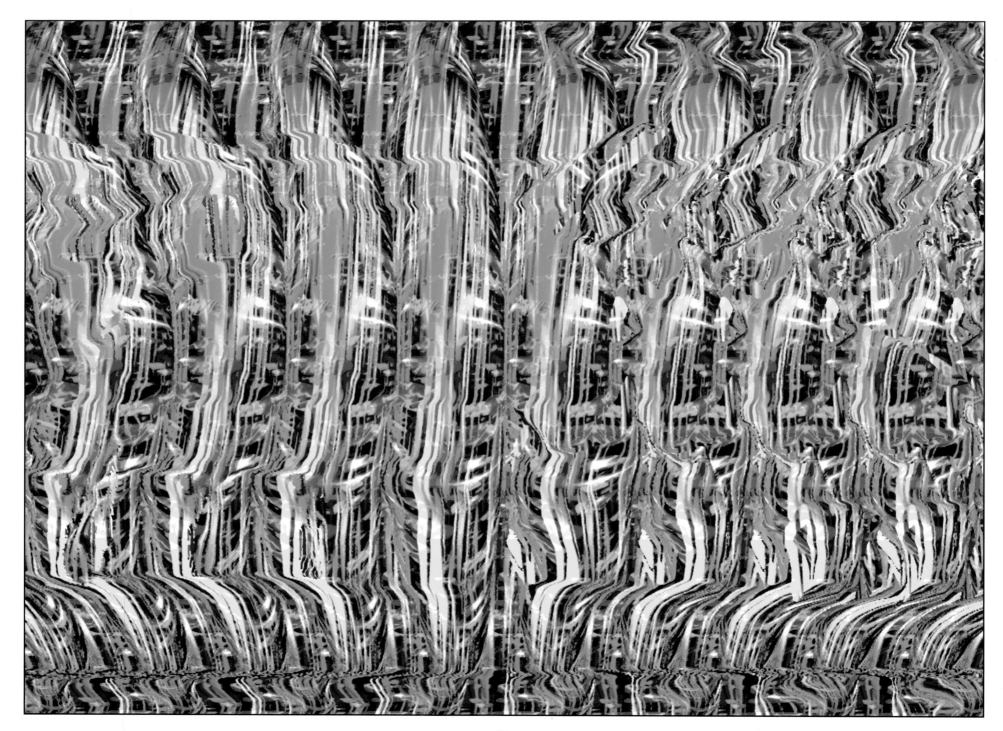

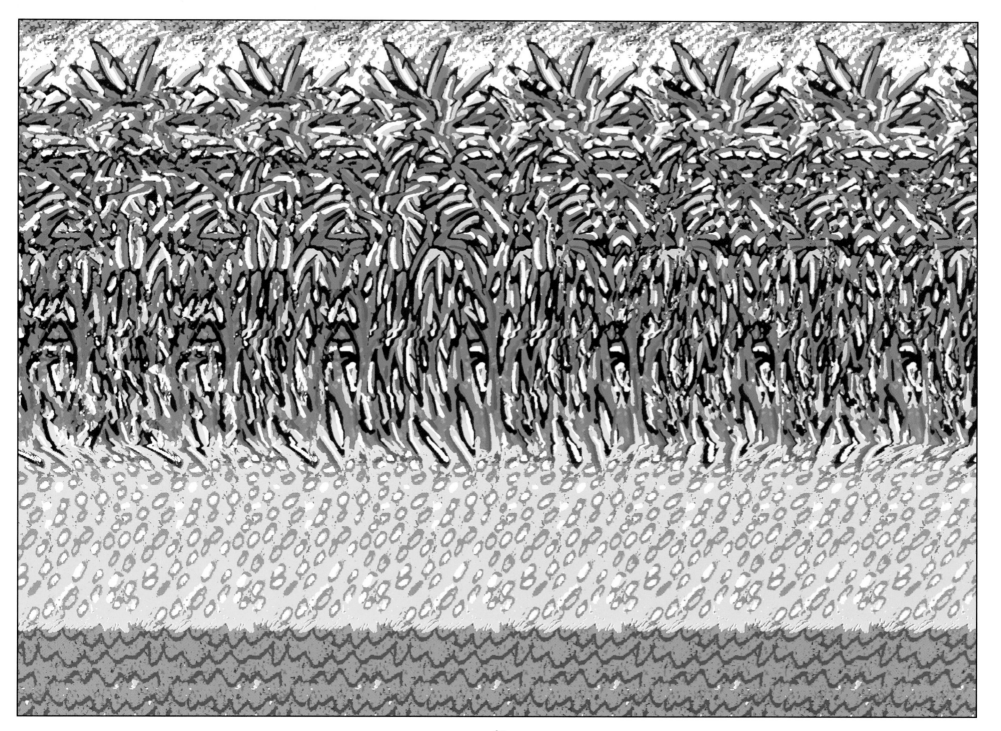

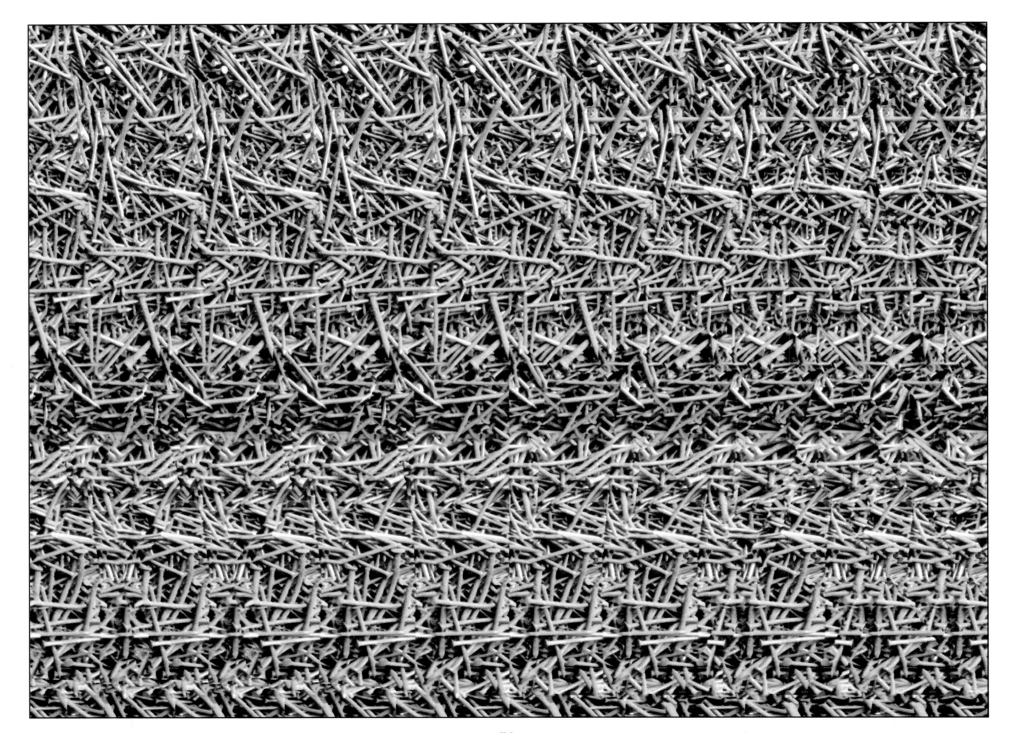

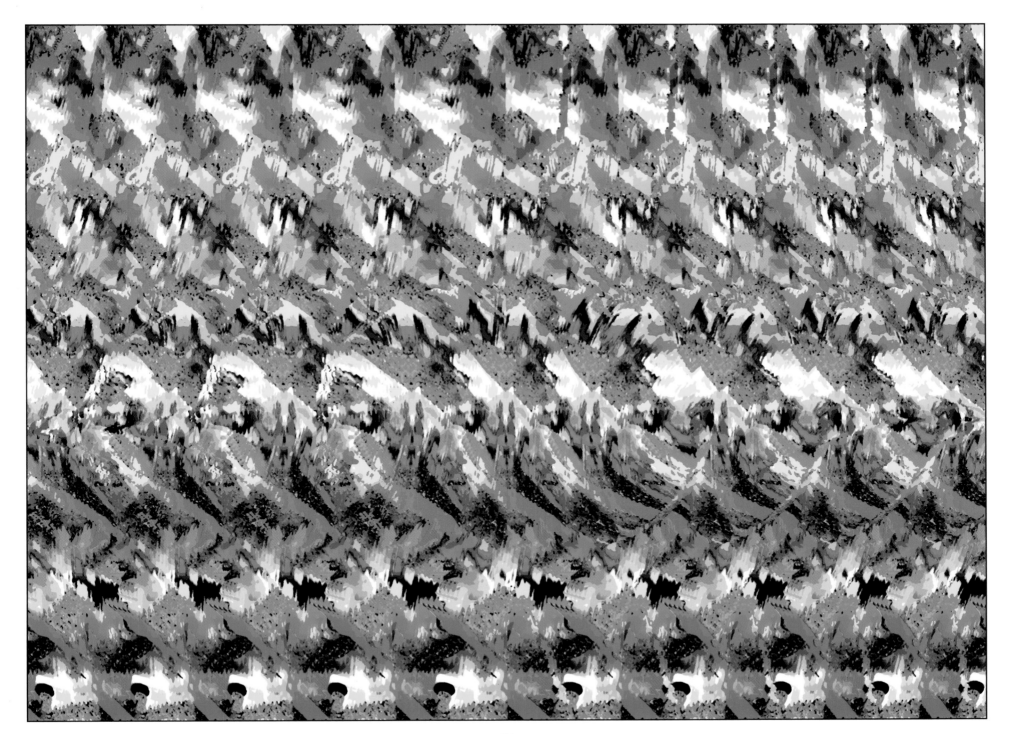

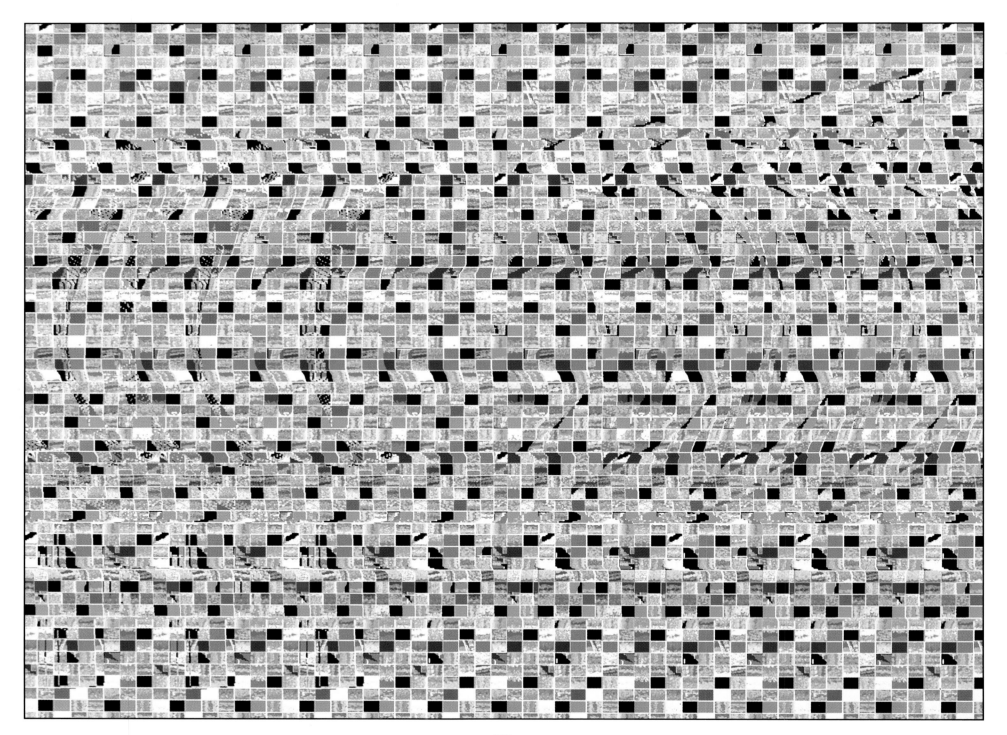

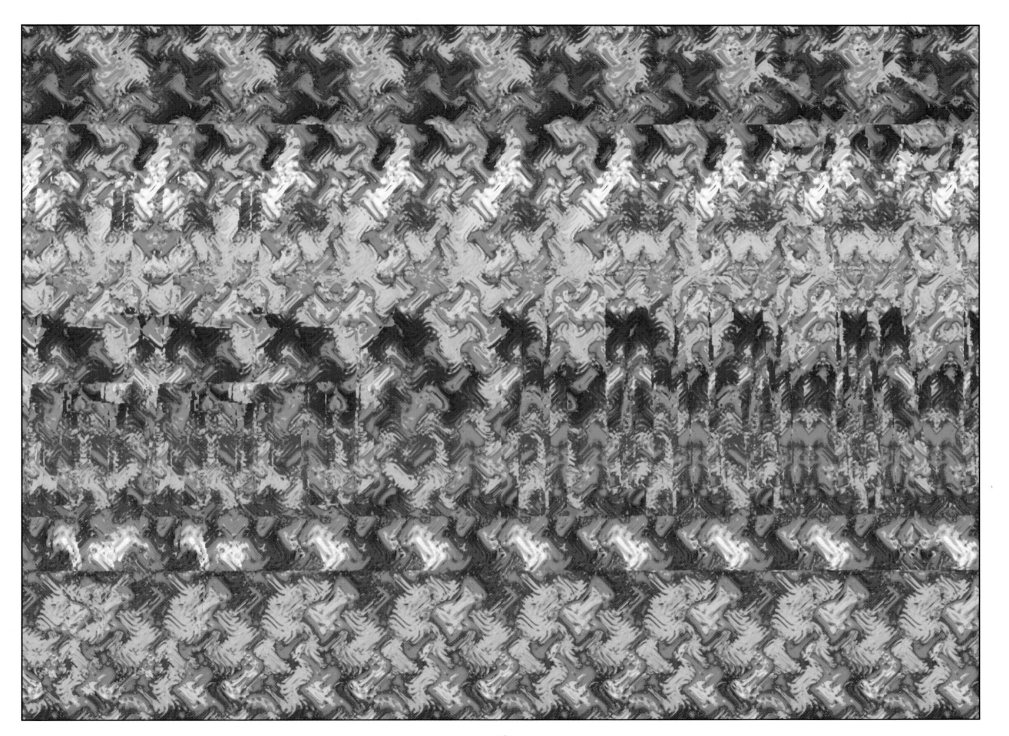

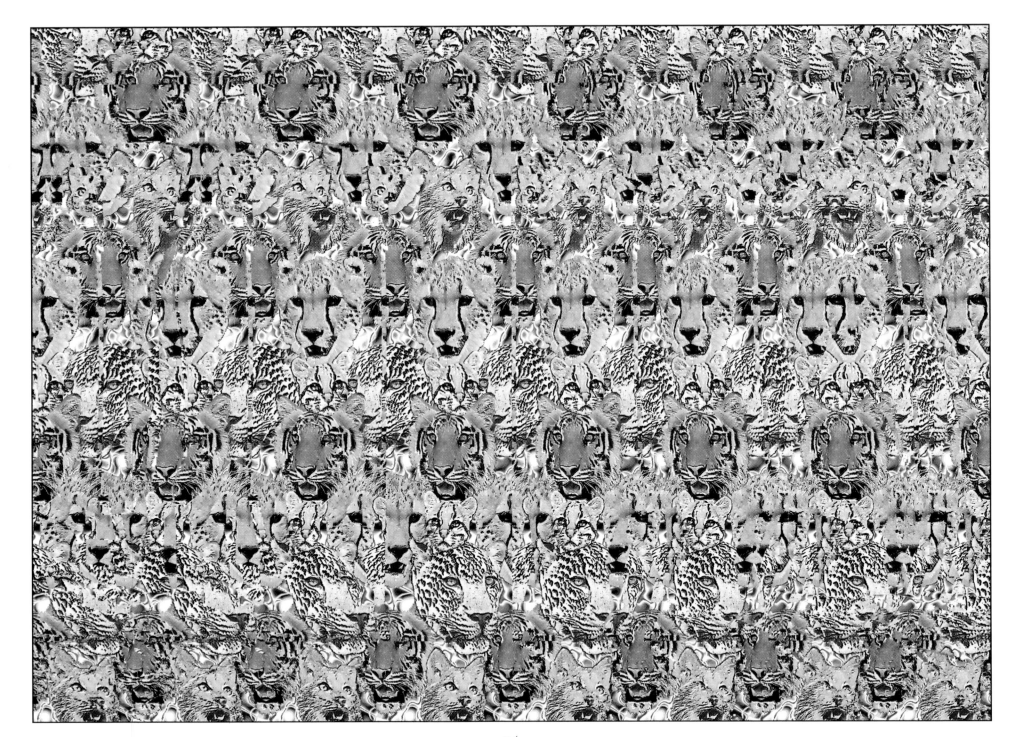

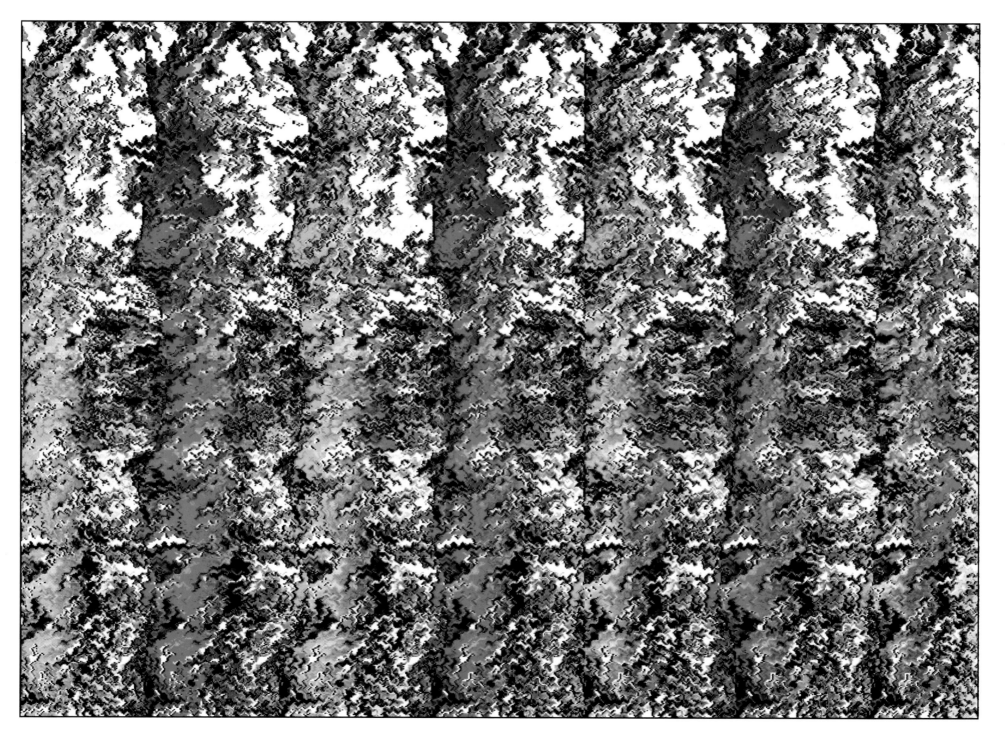

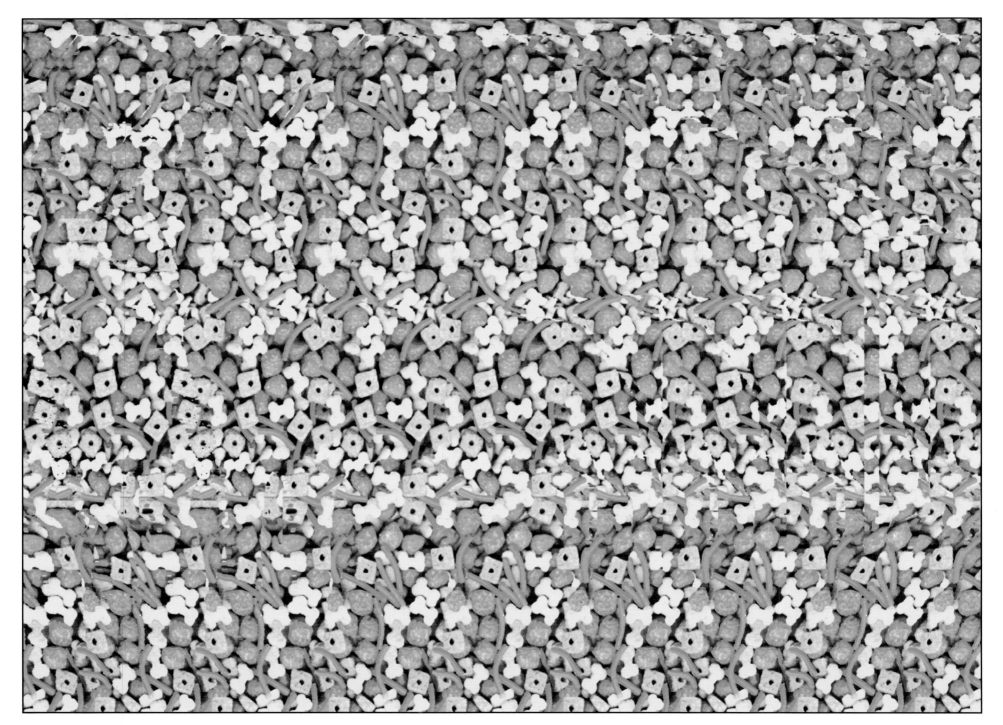

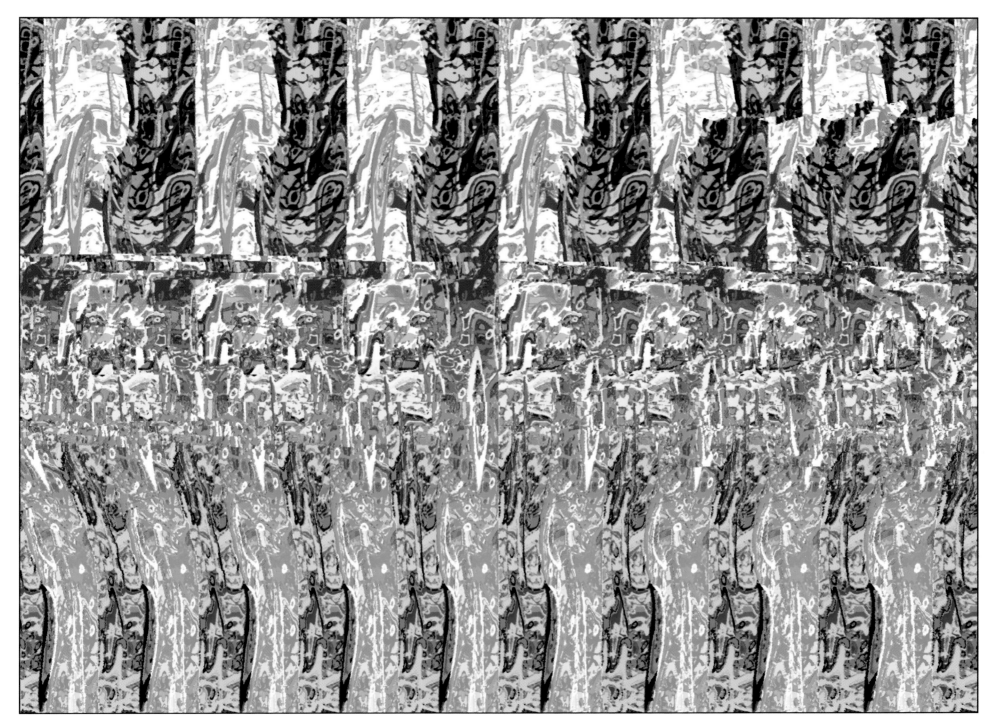

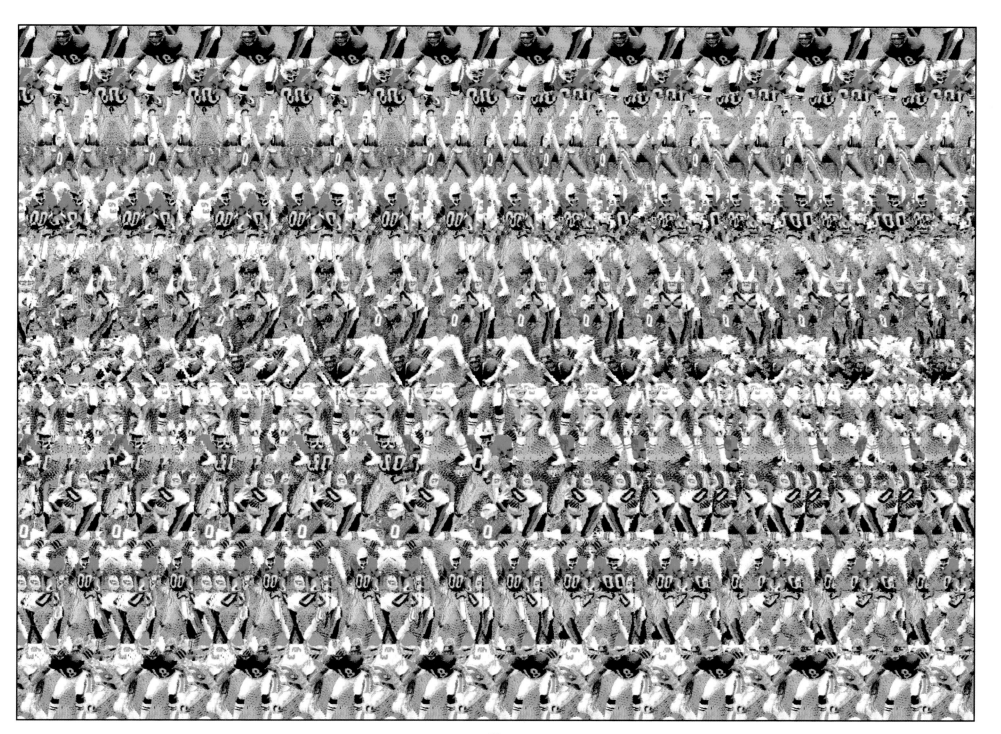

79

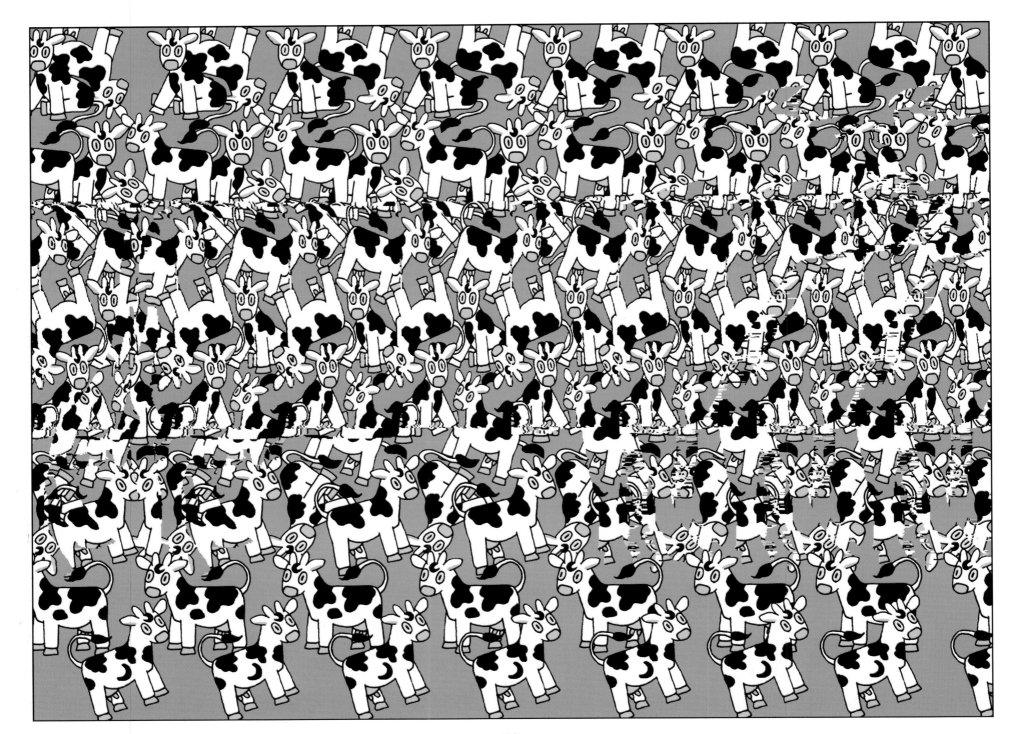

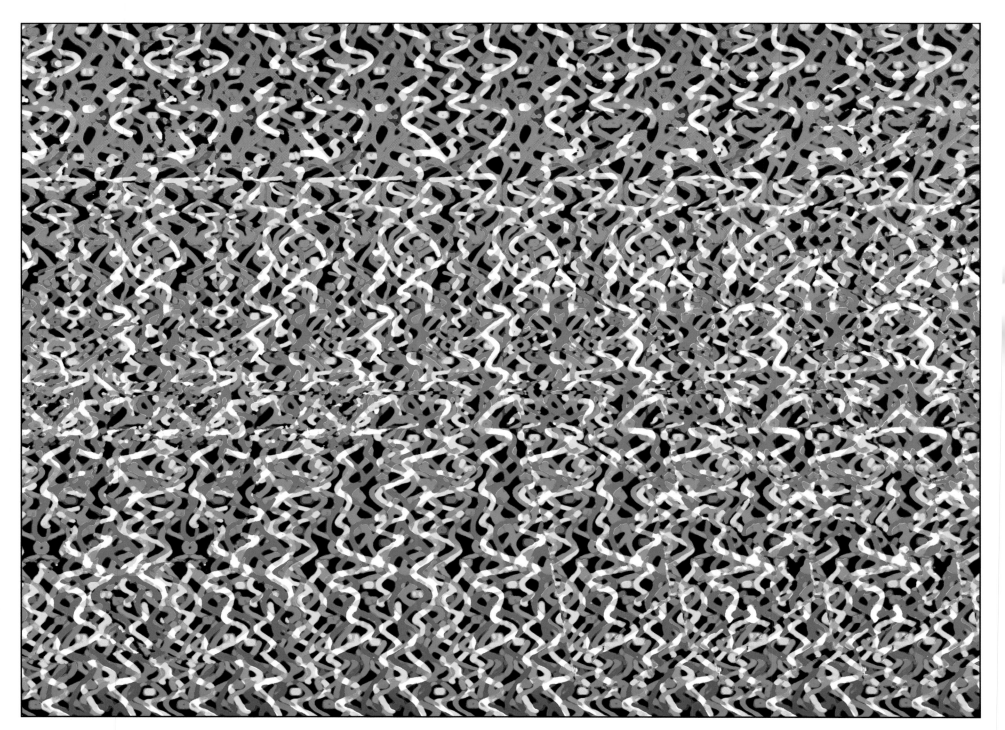

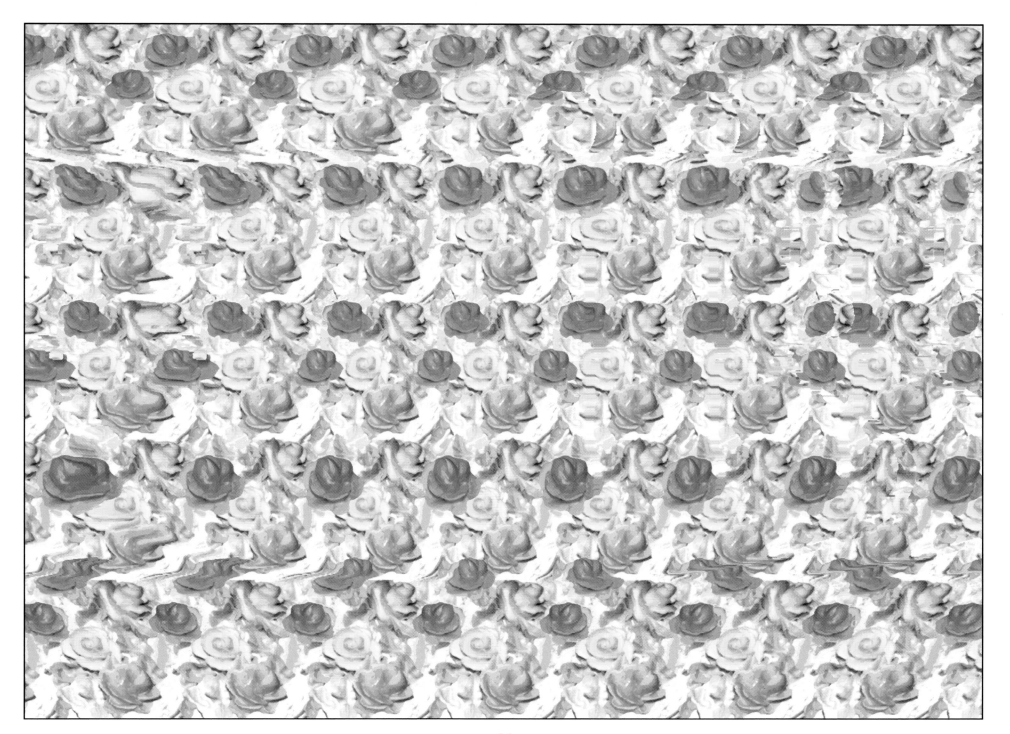

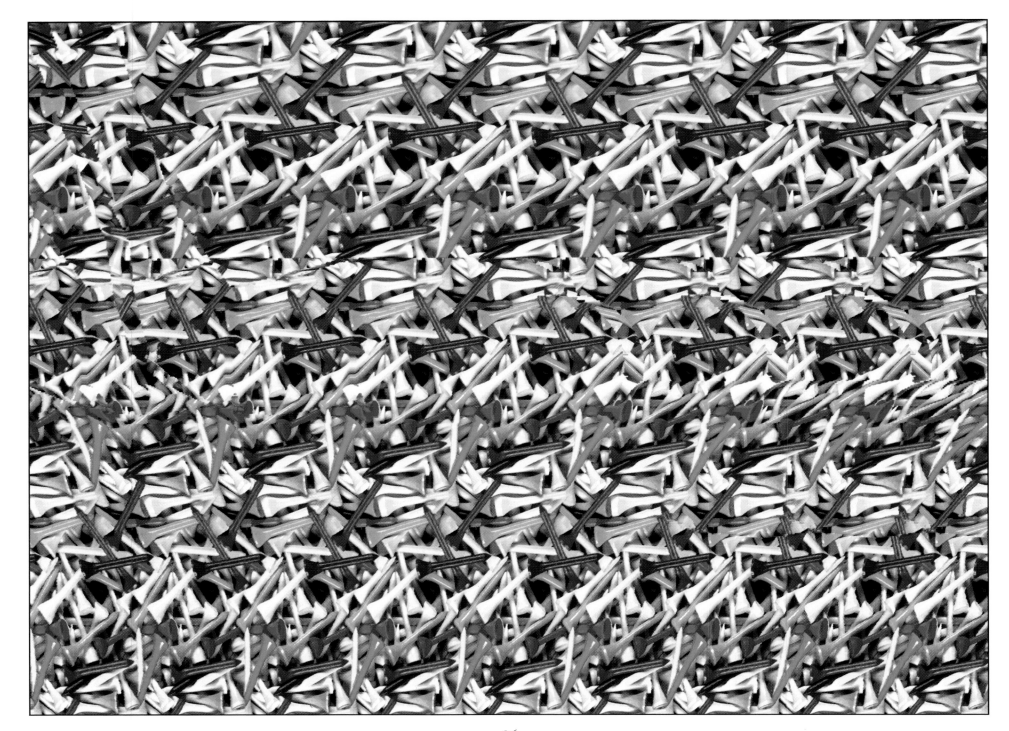

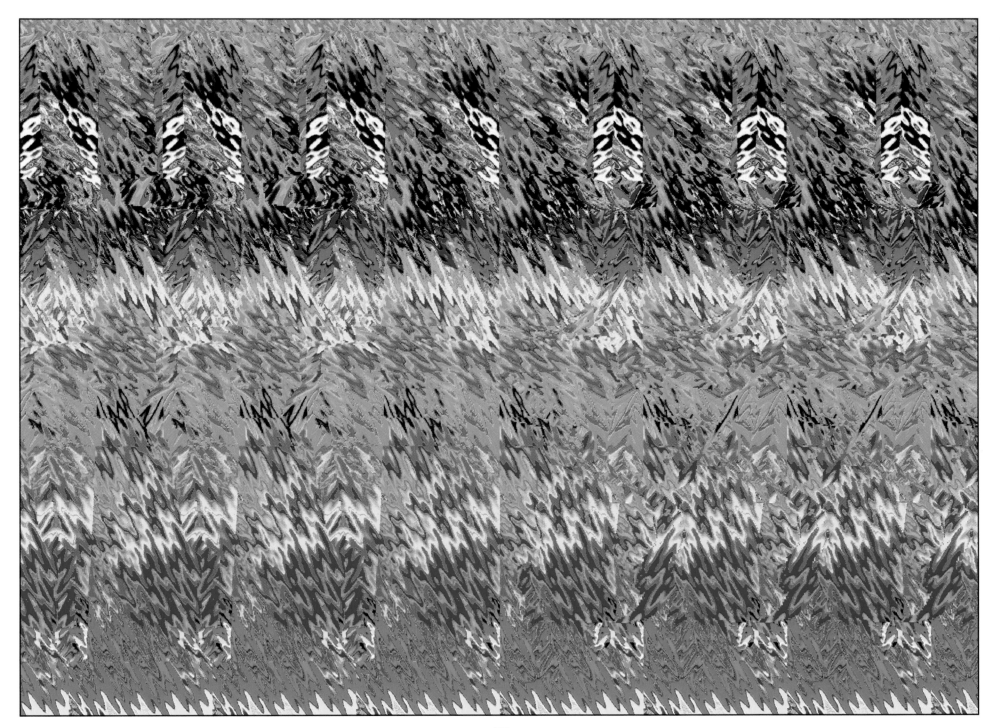

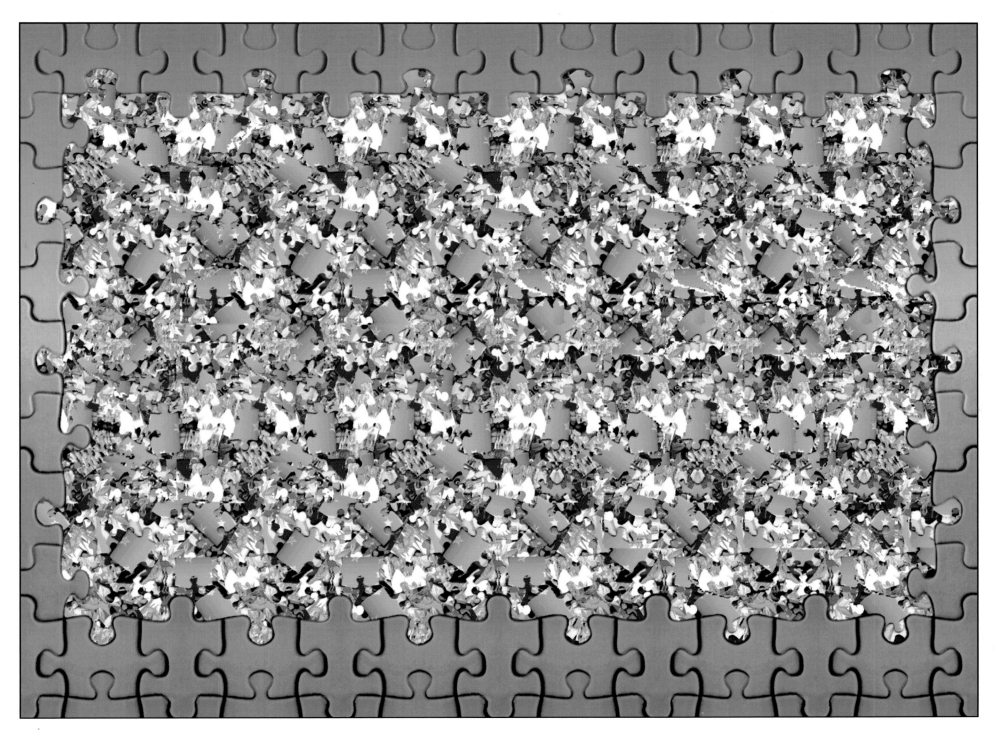

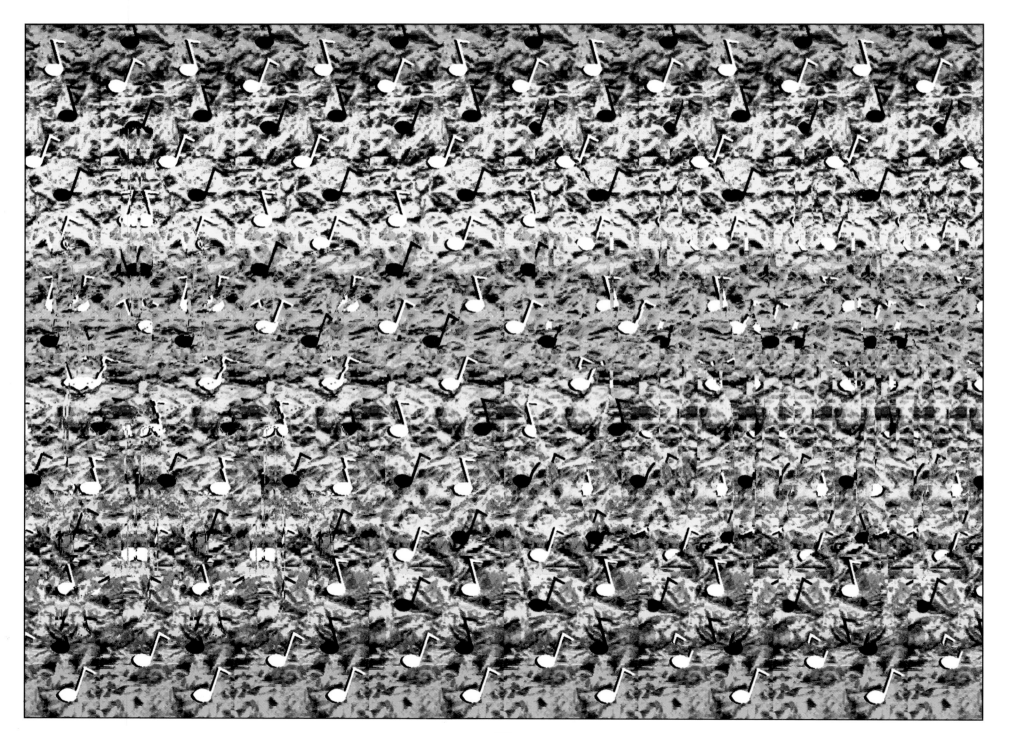

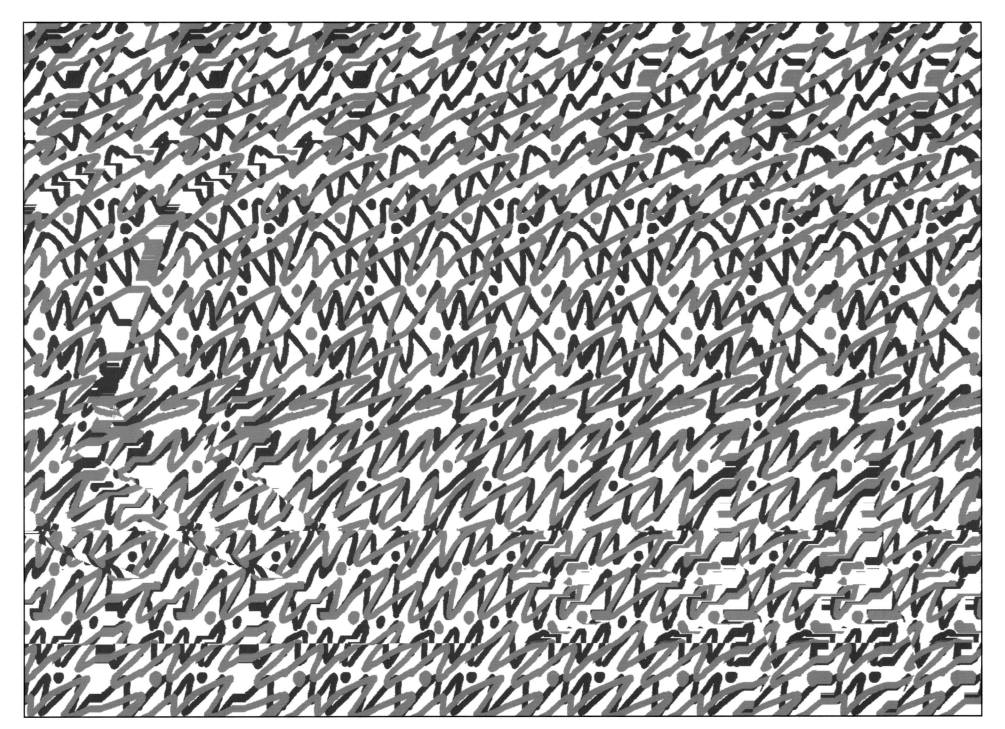

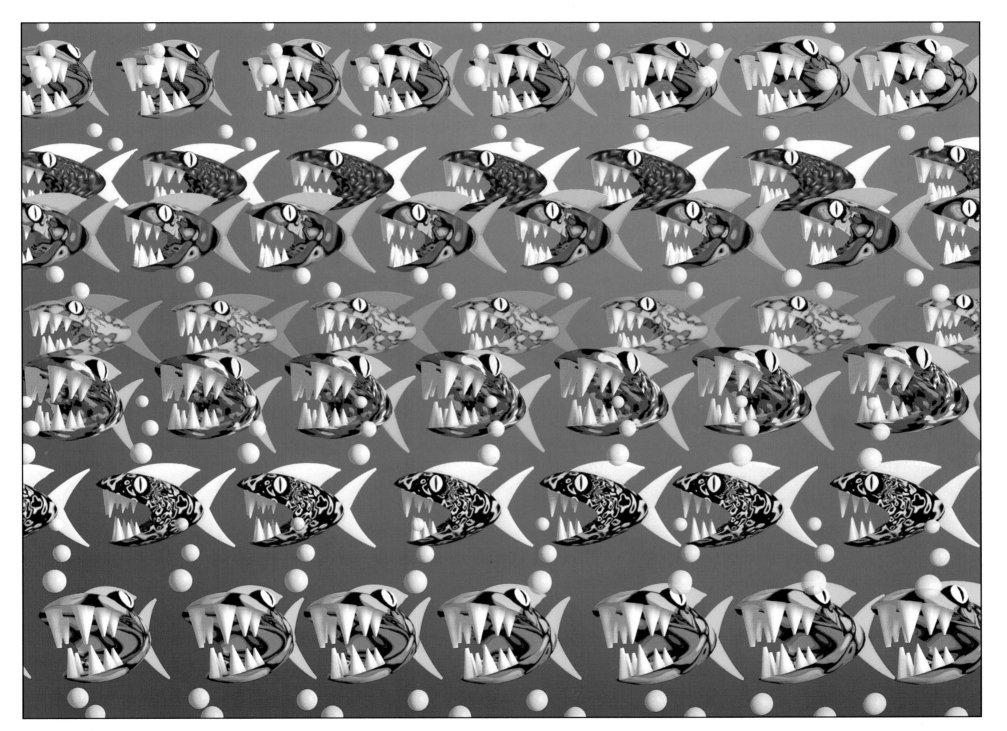

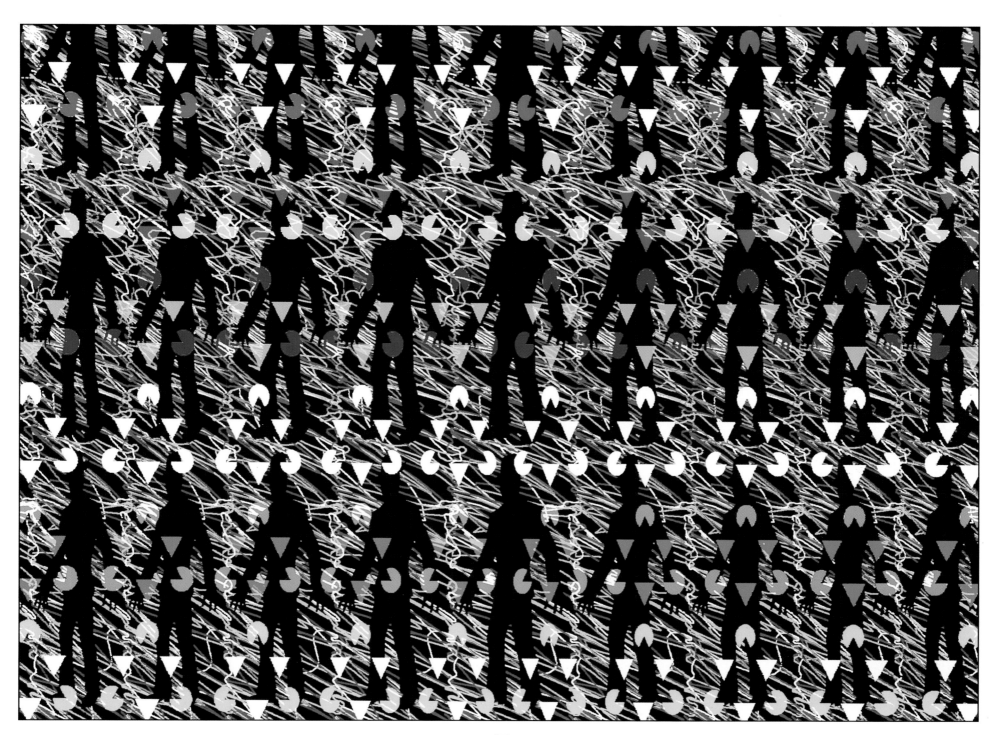

97

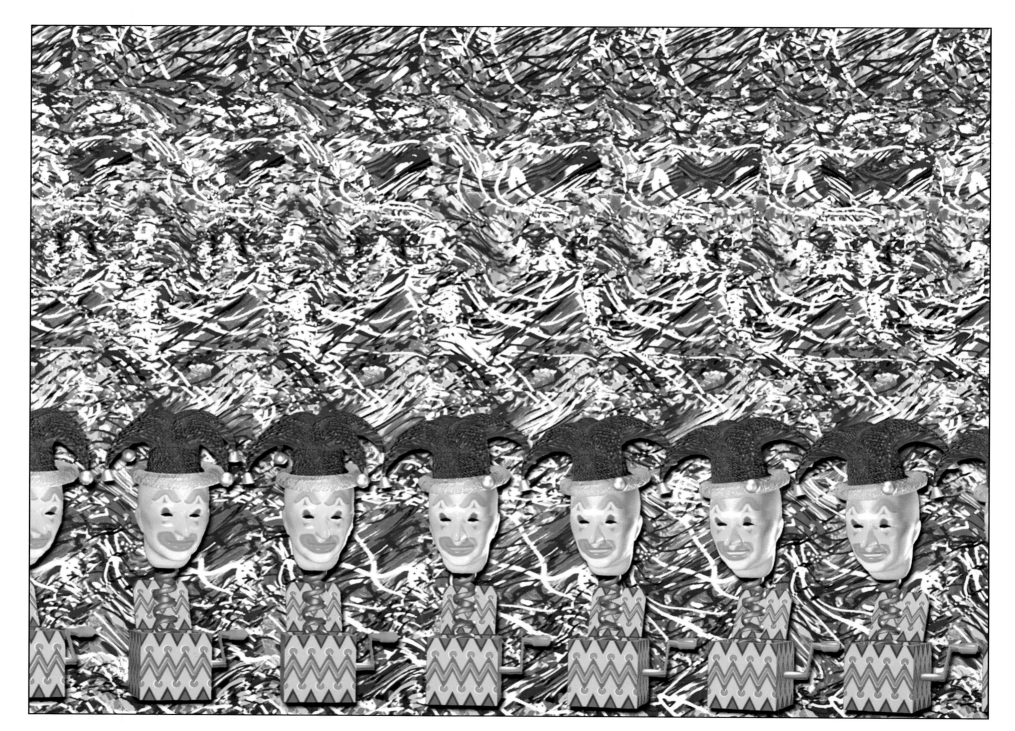

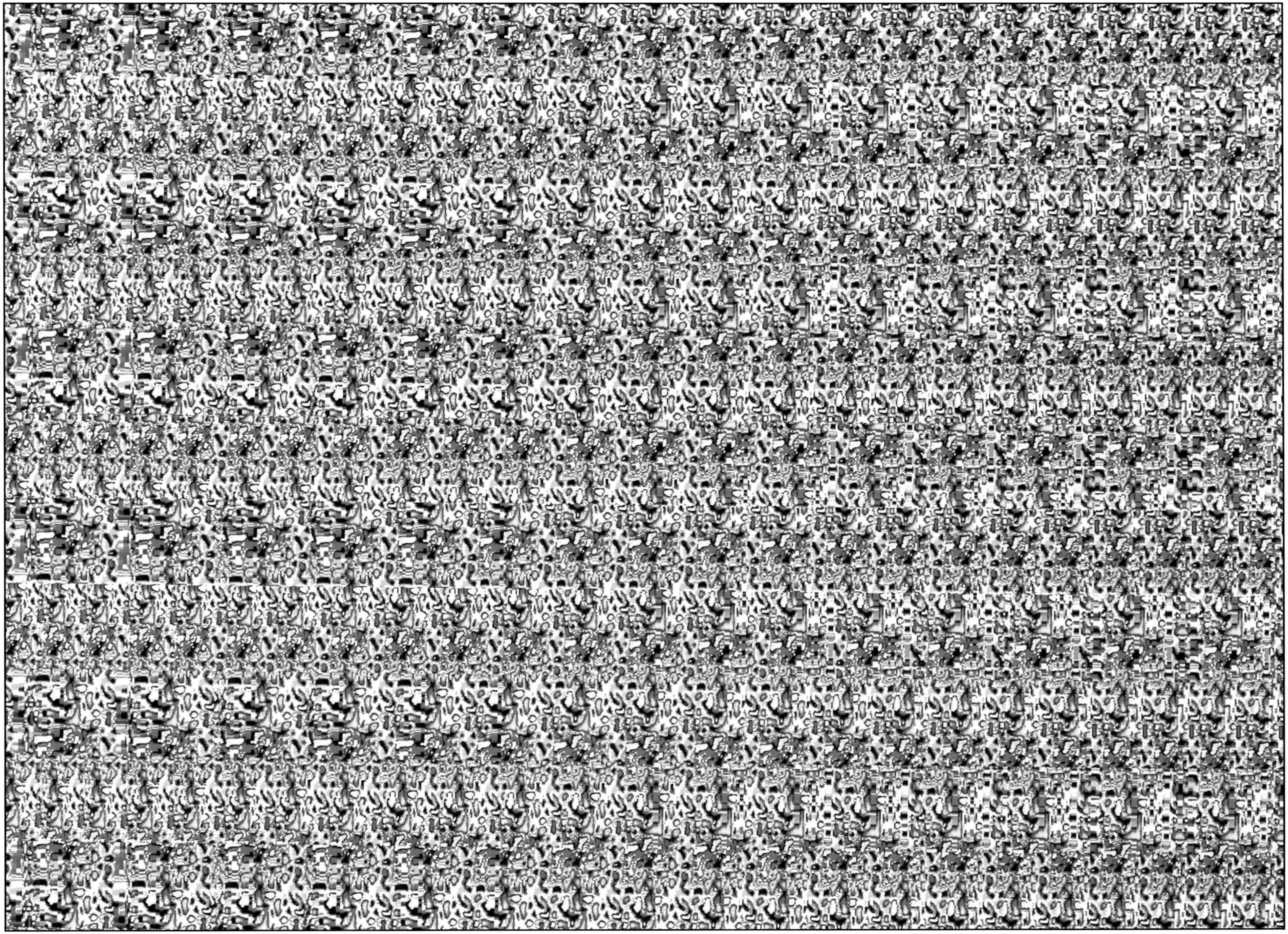

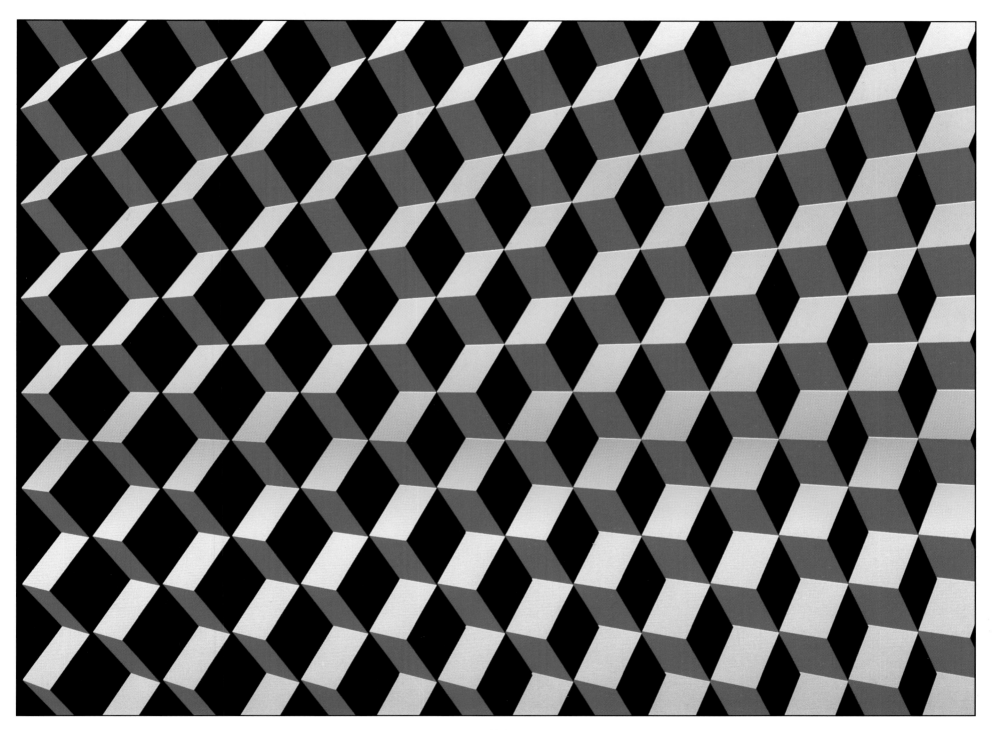

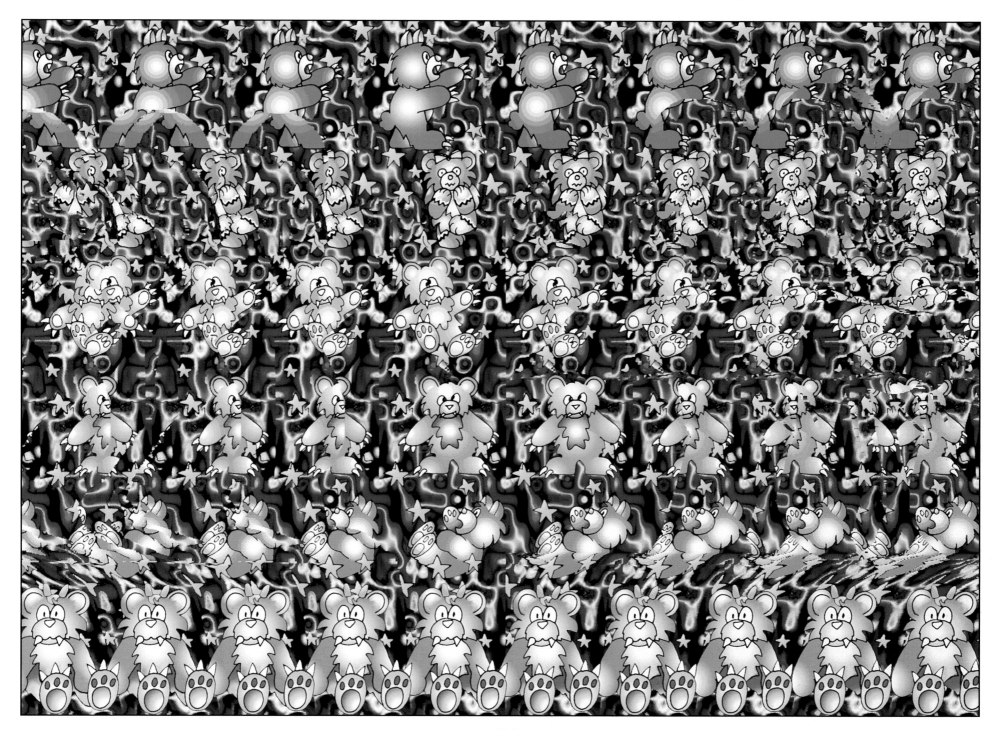

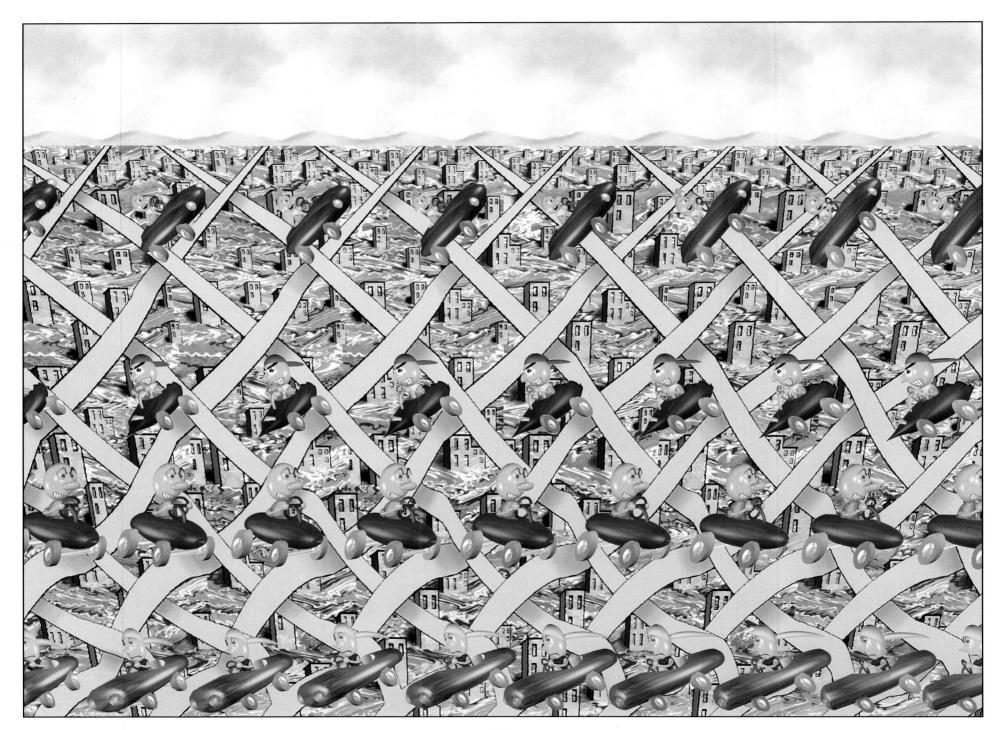

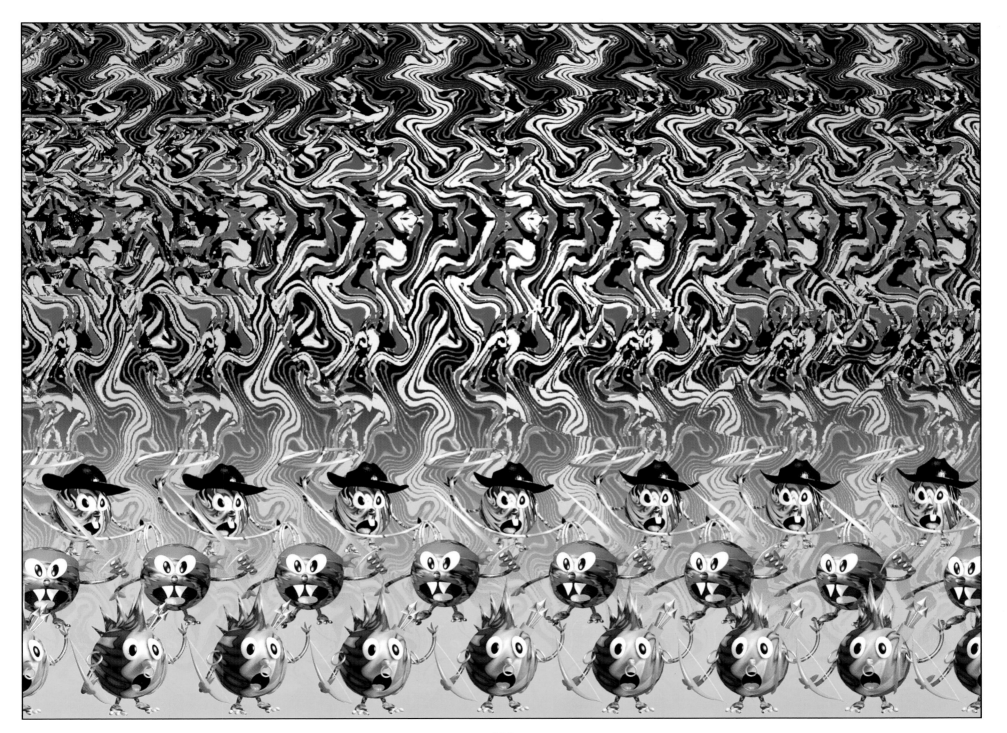

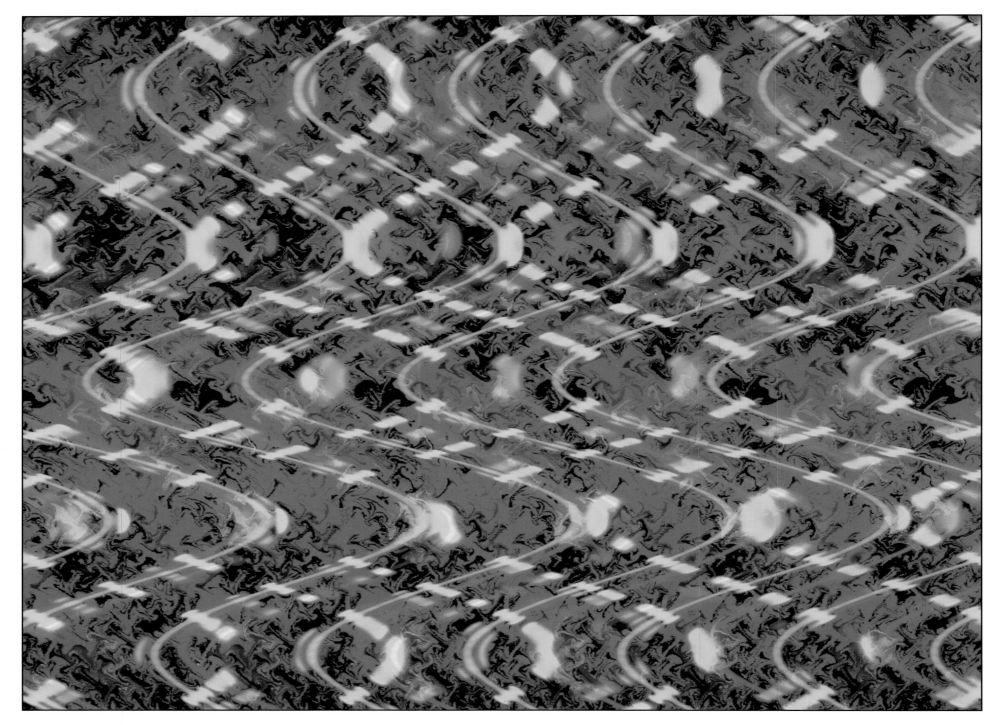

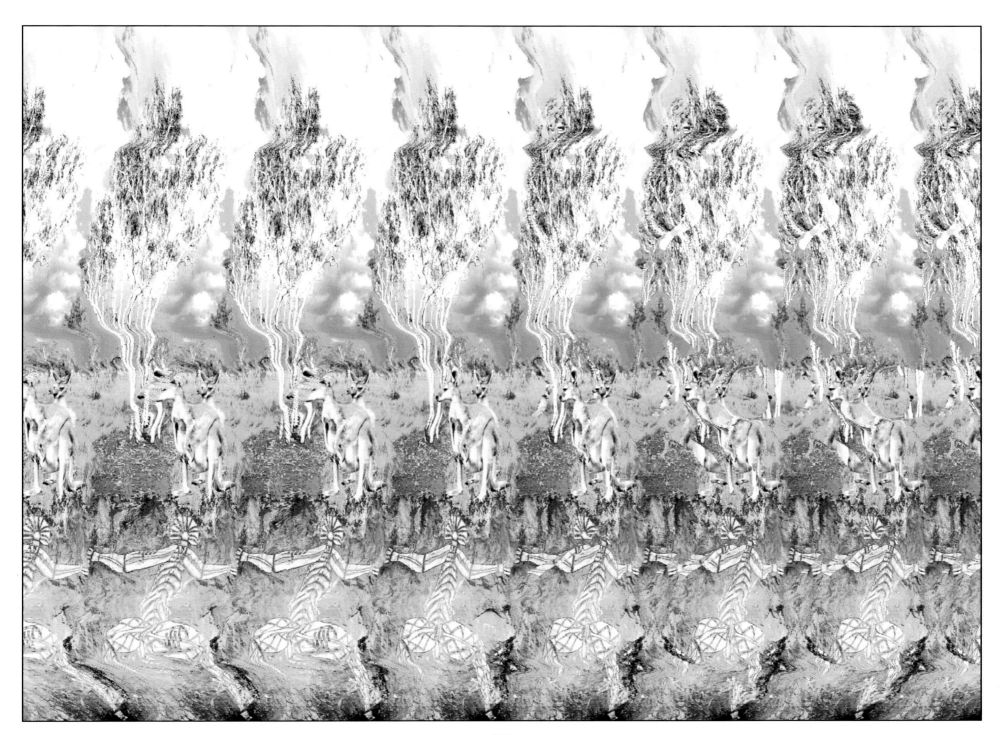

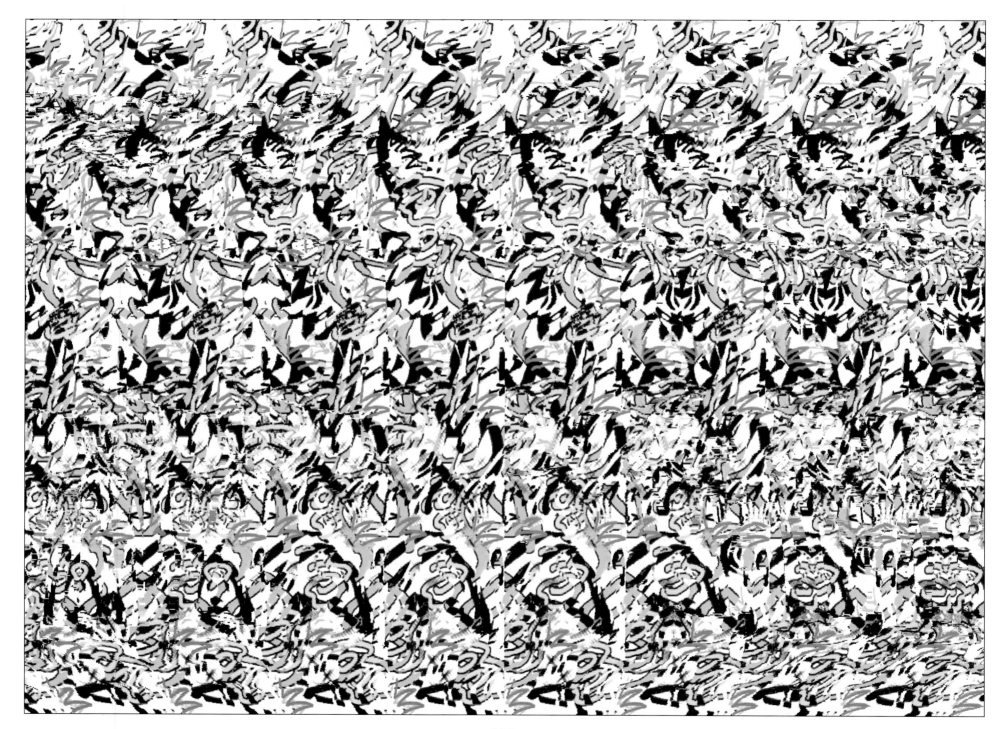

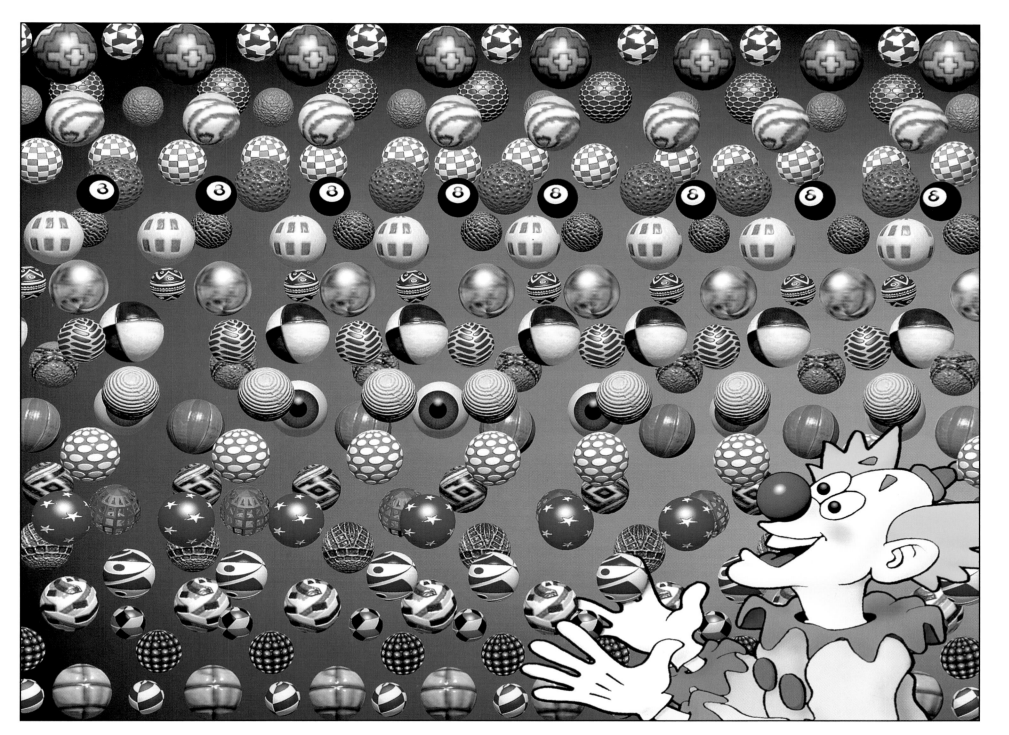

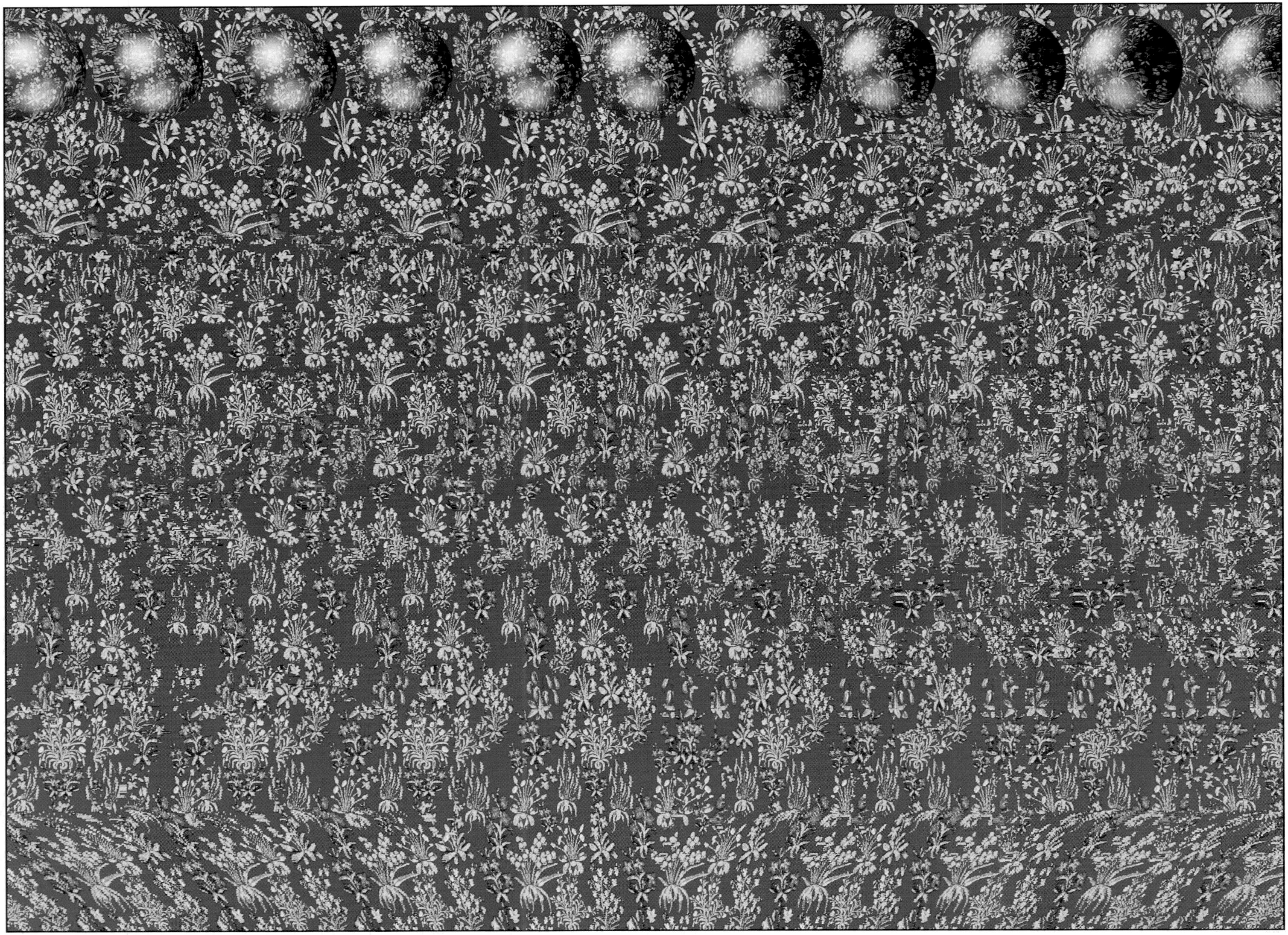

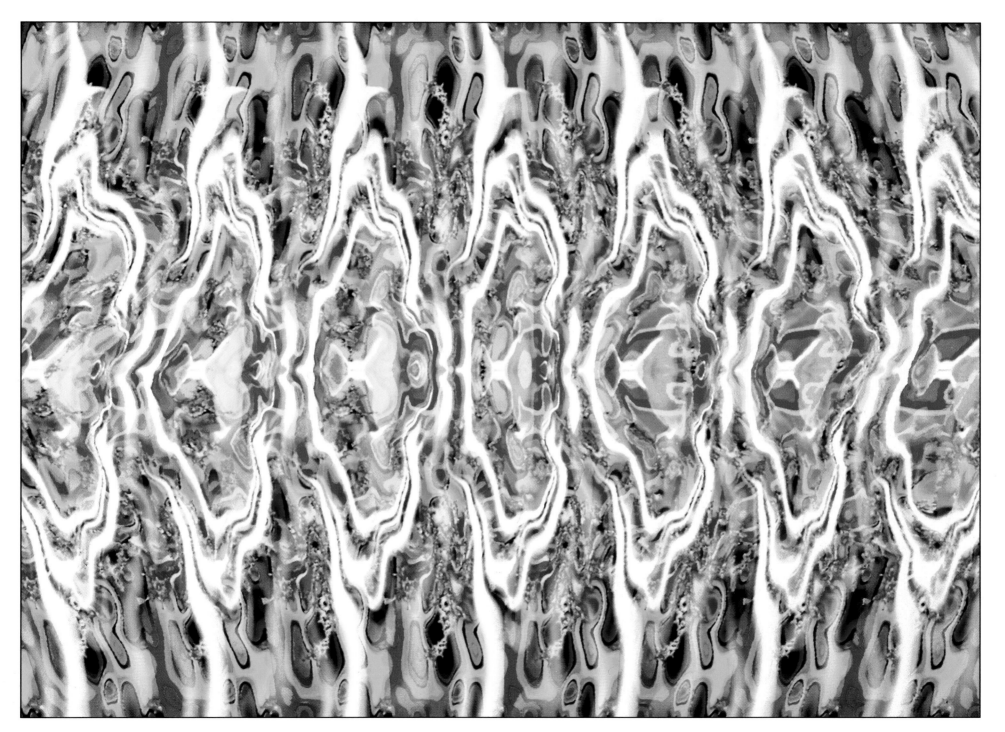

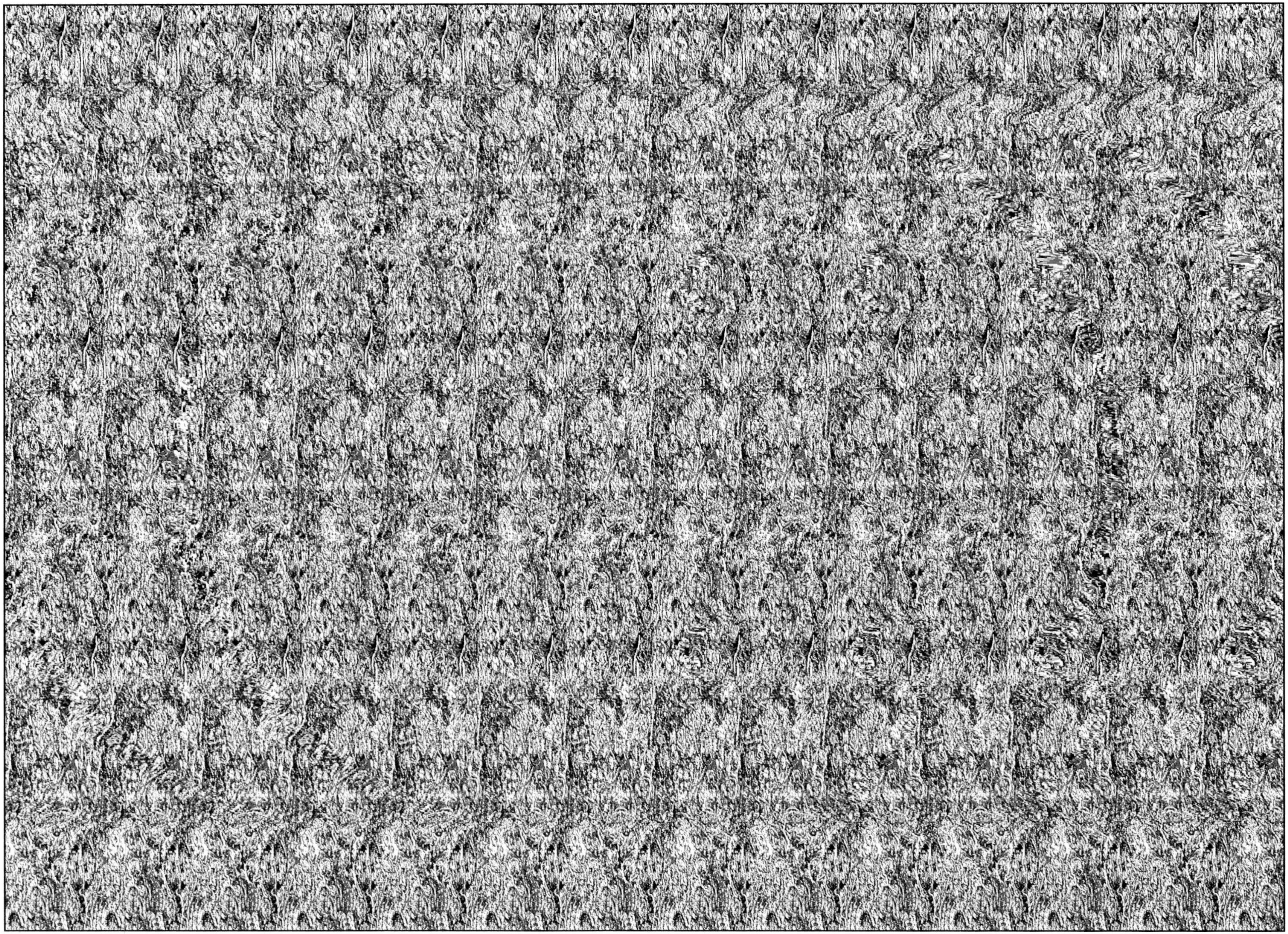

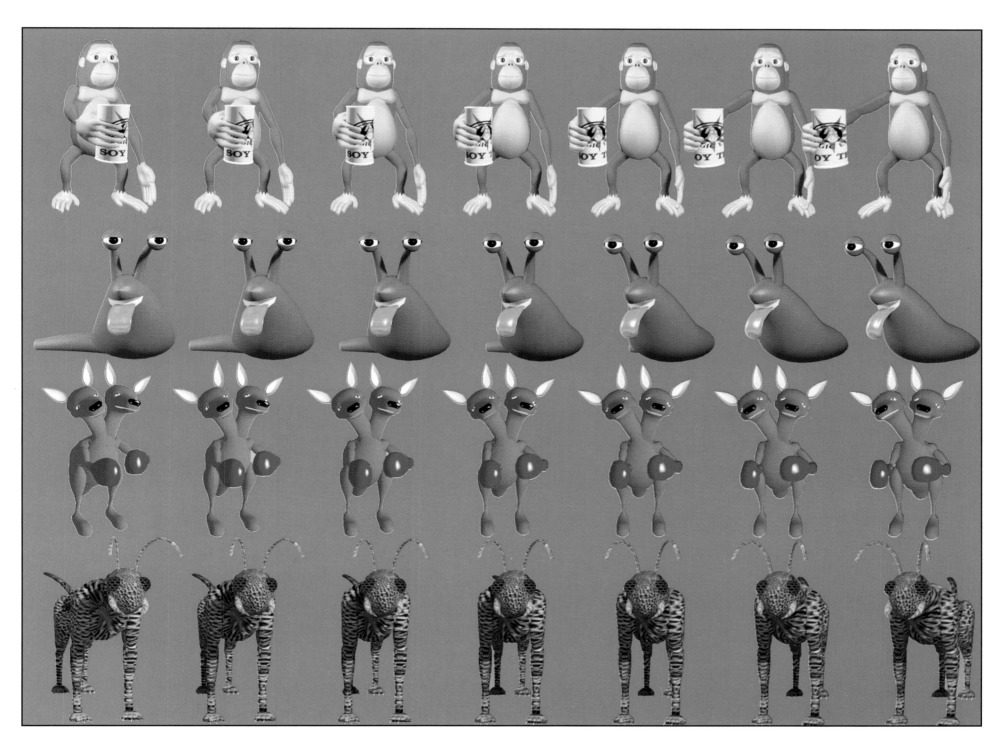

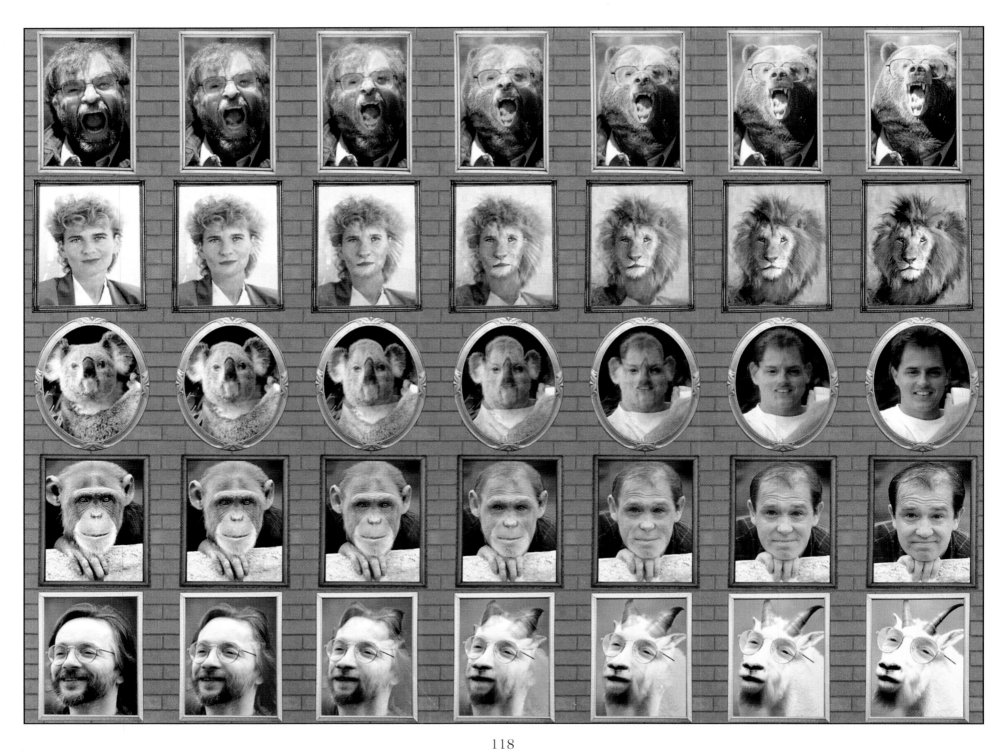

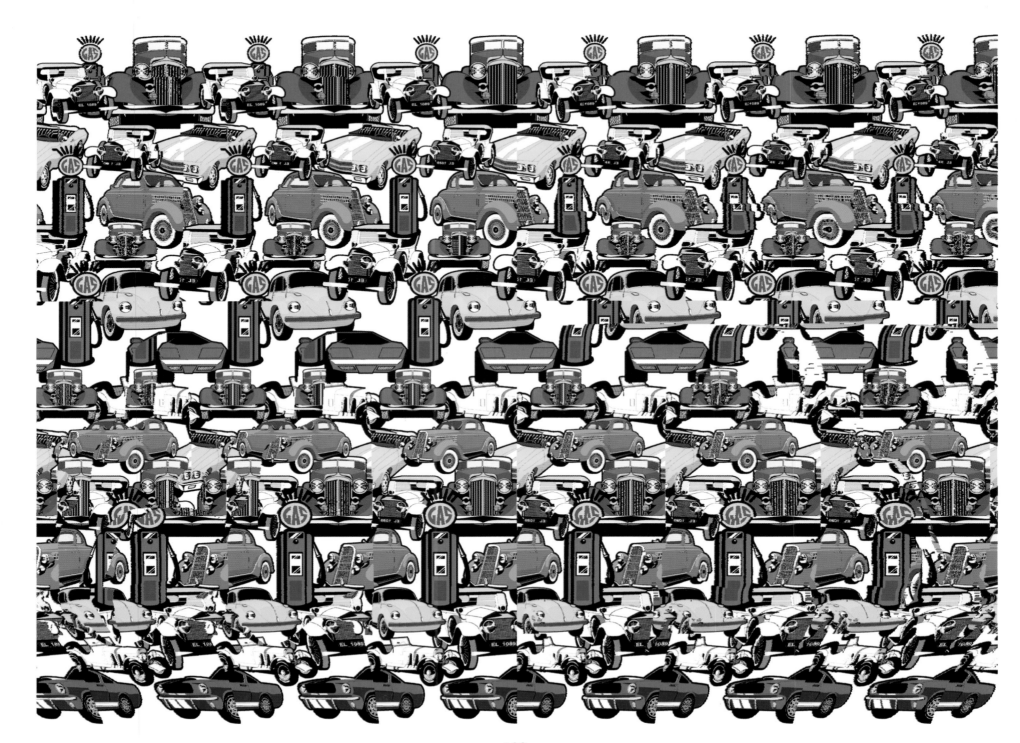

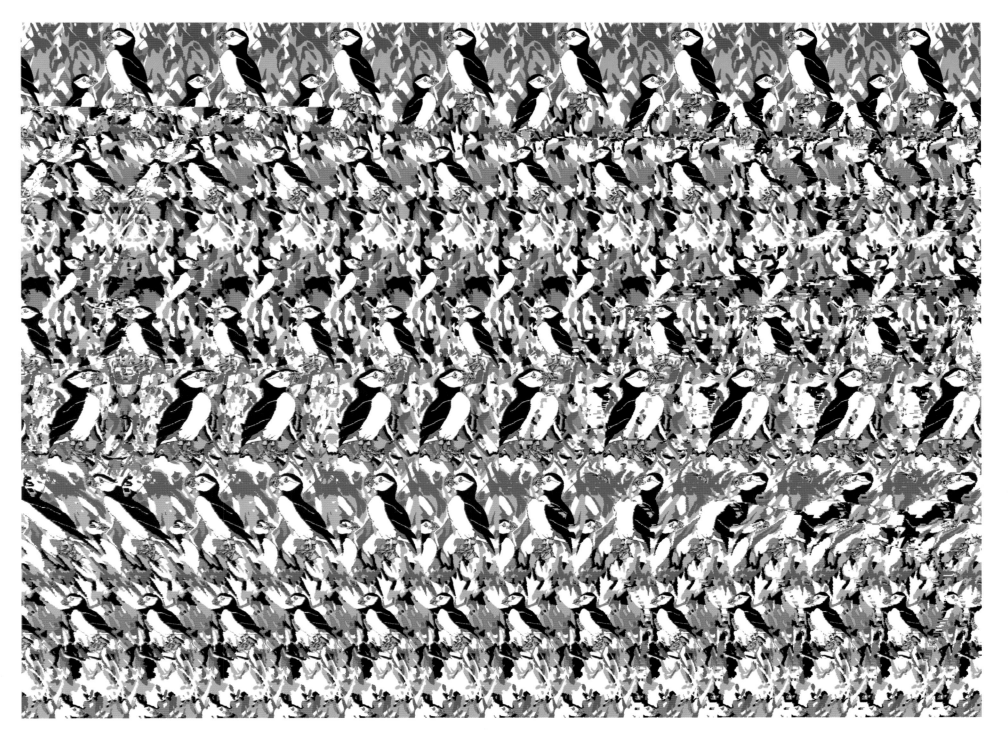

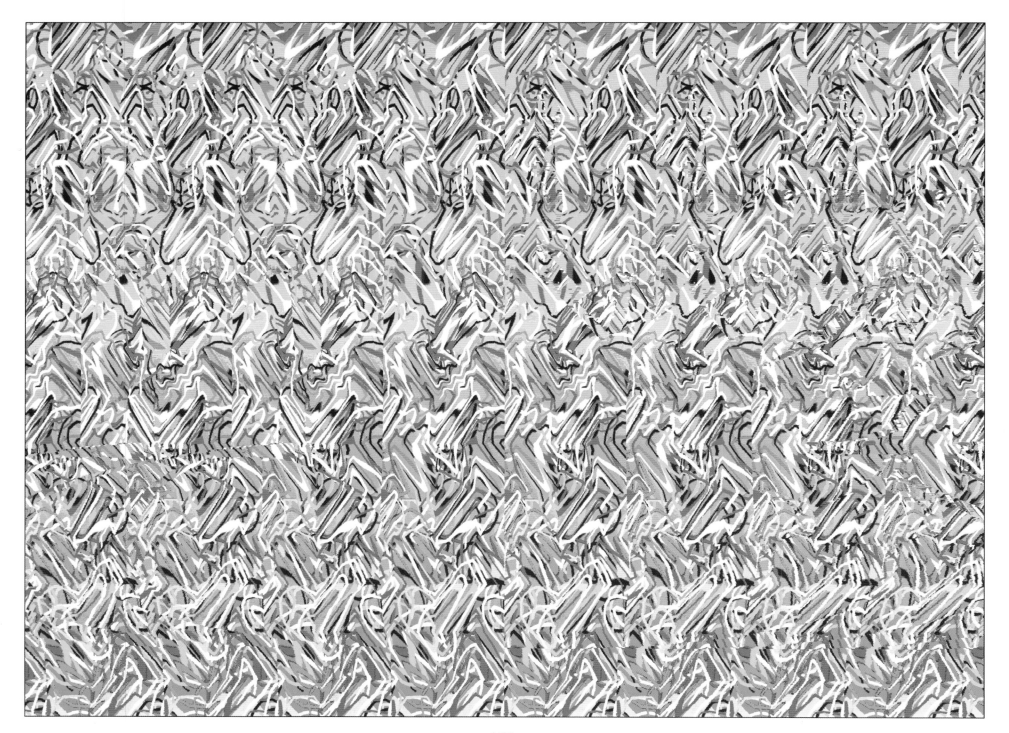

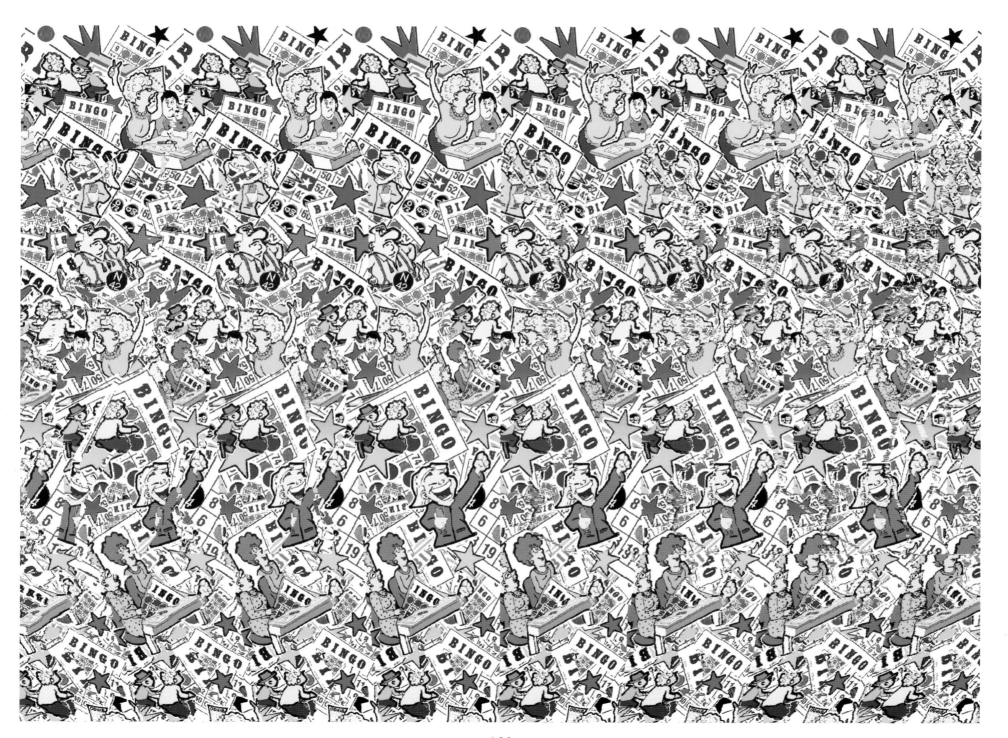

123

Page 5 Window
Page 6 (No image)

Page 7 Buffalo

Page 8 Turtle Cove

Page 9 Biplane

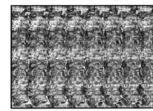

Page 10 Glass 1

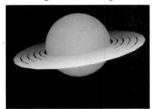

Page 11 Comet Diner

Page 12 The Cookie Knows

Page 13 Chariot

Page 14 Mermaid

Page 15 XXOO

Page 16 Pegasus

Page 17 Target

Page 18 Maze No. 1

Page 19 Amphora

Page 20 Andy's Bunny

Page 21 Shells

Page 22 Cube

Page 23 Jungle

Page 24 Lost in Space

Page 25 Light Rain

Page 26 Rings

Page 27 Liftoff

Page 28 Motorcycle

Page 29 Galleon

Page 30 Dinosaurs

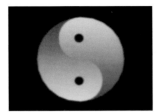

Page 31 Yin Yang

Page 32 Golden Gate

Page 33 Wings

Page 34 Speed

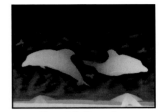

Page 35 Penguins

Page 36 Skydiver

Page 37 Glass 2

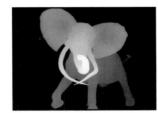

Page 38 Peanut

Page 39 Palm Trees

Page 40 Rockin' Horse

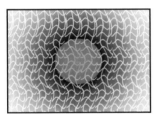

Page 41 Mesh Ball

Page 42 Picnic Bears
Page 43 (No image)

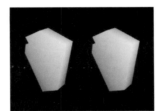

Page 44 Block Heads

Page 45 Cherubs
Page 46 (No image)

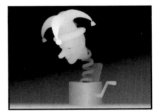

Page 47 Jack-in-the-Box

Page 48 Myopia

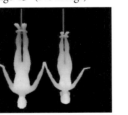

Page 49 Hanging

Page 50 Swirlpool

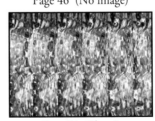

Page 51 Glass 3

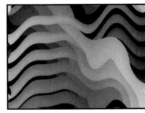

Page 52 Wavy
Page 53 (No image)

Page 54 Corner Pocket

Page 55 Zebra

Page 56 Batty Castle

Page 57 Chopper

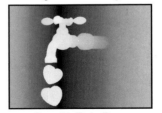

Page 58 Drip Drop

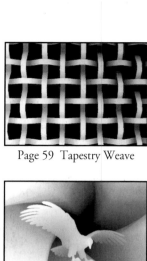

Page 59 Tapestry Weave

Page 60 Surfer

Page 61 Balloon Ride

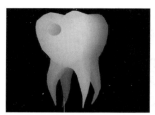

Page 62 Starball

Page 63 Sweet Tooth

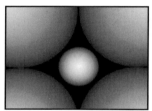

Page 64 Eagle

Page 65 Springs

Page 66 Op Art 8

Page 67 Slam

Page 68 Triceratops

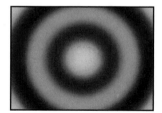

Page 69 Palm Beach

Page 70 Nailed

Page 71 Ugly Cone

Page 72 Relationship

Page 73 Maze No. 2

Page 74 Roar

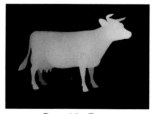

Page 75 Disappear

Page 76 Killer

Page 77 Wolfy

Page 78 Igloo

Page 79 Final Stand

Page 80 Tom's Flower
Page 81 (No image)

Page 82 Cows

Page 83 Sunken Ship

Page 84 New Year's

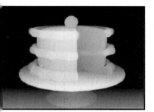

Pages 85 Have Your Cake

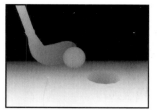

Page 86 Golf Tease

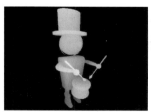

Page 87 Toy Drummer

Page 88 Go van Gogh

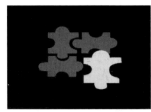

Page 89 Puzzled

Page 90 Sing-along

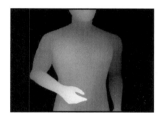

Page 91 Torso

Page 92 Strike

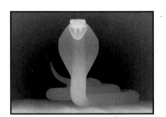

Page 94 King of the Cave

Page 96 Ocean Light

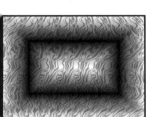

Page 100 Inside Out

Page 101 Land of Myths

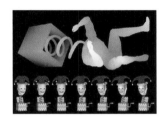

Page 102 What's in the Box?

Page 106 Troo Luv

Page 107 Mutant Teddy

Page 109 Madmarbles

Page 111 The Outback

Page 112 Ribbit

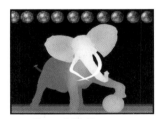

Page 114 Tapestry

Page 116 The Second
Convergence

Page 119 19th Century
Toy

Page 120 3D Roadster

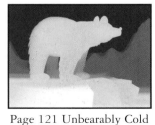

Page 121 Unbearably Cold

Page 122 Which Came First?

Page 123 Bingo

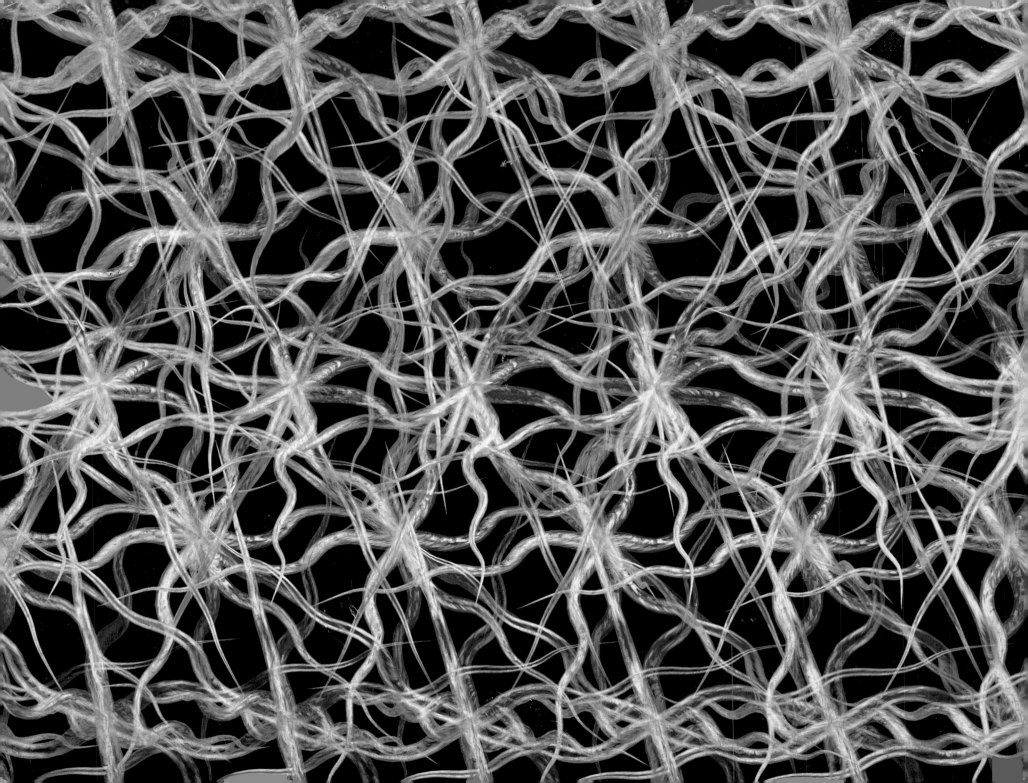